Implementing Cloud Design Patterns for AWS
Second Edition

Solutions and design ideas for solving system design problems

Sean Keery
Clive Harber
Marcus Young

BIRMINGHAM - MUMBAI

Implementing Cloud Design Patterns for AWS
Second Edition

Copyright © 2019 Packt Publishing

All rights reserved. No part of this book may be reproduced, stored in a retrieval system, or transmitted in any form or by any means, without the prior written permission of the publisher, except in the case of brief quotations embedded in critical articles or reviews.

Every effort has been made in the preparation of this book to ensure the accuracy of the information presented. However, the information contained in this book is sold without warranty, either express or implied. Neither the authors, nor Packt Publishing or its dealers and distributors, will be held liable for any damages caused or alleged to have been caused directly or indirectly by this book.

Packt Publishing has endeavored to provide trademark information about all of the companies and products mentioned in this book by the appropriate use of capitals. However, Packt Publishing cannot guarantee the accuracy of this information.

Commissioning Editor: Vijin Boricha
Acquisition Editor: Shrilekha Inani
Content Development Editor: Nithin George Varghese
Technical Editor: Komal Karne
Copy Editor: Safis Editing
Project Coordinator: Jagdish Prabhu
Proofreader: Safis Editing
Indexer: Rekha Nair
Graphics: Tom Scaria
Production Coordinator: Shraddha Falebhai

First published: April 2015
Second edition: April 2019

Production reference: 1300419

Published by Packt Publishing Ltd.
Livery Place
35 Livery Street
Birmingham
B3 2PB, UK.

ISBN 978-1-78913-620-3

www.packtpub.com

This book is dedicated to my wonderful wife, Leslie, and my son, Haven; without their support through the weekends and late nights, I would not have been able to persevere.

– Sean Keery

Dedicated to my family and all those who believed.

– Clive Harber

`mapt.io`

Mapt is an online digital library that gives you full access to over 5,000 books and videos, as well as industry leading tools to help you plan your personal development and advance your career. For more information, please visit our website.

Why subscribe?

- Spend less time learning and more time coding with practical eBooks and Videos from over 4,000 industry professionals
- Improve your learning with Skill Plans built especially for you
- Get a free eBook or video every month
- Mapt is fully searchable
- Copy and paste, print, and bookmark content

Packt.com

Did you know that Packt offers eBook versions of every book published, with PDF and ePub files available? You can upgrade to the eBook version at `www.packt.com` and as a print book customer, you are entitled to a discount on the eBook copy. Get in touch with us at `customercare@packtpub.com` for more details.

At `www.packt.com`, you can also read a collection of free technical articles, sign up for a range of free newsletters, and receive exclusive discounts and offers on Packt books and eBooks.

Contributors

About the authors

Sean Keery began hacking obscure video game systems at the age of 13. Sean then developed interpersonal skills while teaching snowboarding. Nowadays, Cloud Foundry, choreography, containers and plenty of .io. Cluster deployments, IaaS independence, and his studies for a master's in data science keep Sean occupied. The daily commute is filled with podcasts and chipmunk bunny hops. Some family time, spicy food, a good book, and wrecking the latest toys keep Sean busy at home.

> *Thanks to my parents and family for providing me with the environment and opportunities to succeed; the Cassetty's for cold beer and a warm fire; Rick Farmer for inspiration; Weems for teaching me how to lead; Joe Szodfridt for helping me develop a product mindset; and Matt Russell and Joe Fitzgerald, who helped me refine my brand. Many thanks also to Duncan Winn, Craig Wheeless, Keith Strini, Matt Brockman, and Haydon Ryan for being my sounding board.*

Clive Harber has been programming computers since he was 13, when Commodore Basic was all the rage and the internet, as an idea, was something that was only just starting to appear in films such as WarGames. Fast-forward a decade, he gained a master's degree in chemical engineering from University of Wales, Swansea, which he used briefly in a stint when he worked in a semi-conductor foundry making microchips. Not being totally satisfied with this, he decided to change fields and learn how to write stuff for the internet. Now, he runs his own consultancy, Distorted Thinking, providing services to organizations that find themselves in digital transition, whether that's software changes or infrastructure to cloud service migration.

> *This book would not have been possible without the patience and support of my family putting up with all the late nights, early mornings, and writer's block. It seems that they have more faith in me than I do in myself. I would also like to thank the editorial and technical staff at Packt for giving me this opportunity. They were also crucial in maintaining some sort of momentum and keeping me on track.*

Marcus Young obtained a degree in computer science and mathematics before getting involved in system administration and DevOps. He currently works in software automation using open source tools and technologies. His hobbies include playing ice hockey and brewing homebrew beer. He also enjoys hardware projects based on microcontrollers and single-board computers.

About the reviewers

Zubin Ghafari is an AWS cloud-certified professional and consultant in cloud engineering and architecture. He currently holds over eight AWS certifications at associate, professional, and specialty levels. With a passion for consulting and the cloud, Zubin enjoys spending his time experimenting and developing customized solutions for the Amazon Web Services cloud platform. He has immense gratitude for his peers at Slalom, who have supported him in his career.

Amado Gramajo is a passionate technologist with over 15 years of experience working for Fortune 100 companies and leading virtualization, platform migrations, and, currently, cloud migrations. He holds multiple AWS certifications at the professional and specialty levels.

Packt is searching for authors like you

If you're interested in becoming an author for Packt, please visit `authors.packtpub.com` and apply today. We have worked with thousands of developers and tech professionals, just like you, to help them share their insight with the global tech community. You can make a general application, apply for a specific hot topic that we are recruiting an author for, or submit your own idea.

Table of Contents

Preface 1

Section 1: The Basics

Chapter 1: Introduction to Amazon Web Services 9
   Introduction to AWS 10
      History 10
      The future 11
         Product 11
         Data 11
         Code 12
      Utility computing 12
         Anything as a Service 12
            Infrastructure as a Service 13
            Platform as a Service 13
            Software as a Service 14
      Cloud continuum 14
         Microservices 15
      Crazy new services 15
      Free trials 16
      Huge catalog 18
         Software defined, API driven 19
         Benefits of moving to the cloud 19
            Software engineer 19
            Operations engineer 20
            Product owner 20
   Summary 21
   Further reading 22

Chapter 2: Core Services - Building Blocks for Your Product ... 23
   Technical requirements 24
   Code 24
      Cloud9 24
      CodeCommit 31
   Compute 32
      Instances 33
         Types 33
         Usage 34
            Shared 34
            Dedicated 34
            Spot or ephemeral 34
      Raw 35
         Containers 35

Table of Contents

Functions	35
Networking	35
Internet Protocol	36
Elastic IP	36
IPv6	36
Route 53	36
DNS	36
Global traffic manager	36
Virtual Private Cloud	37
Subnets	37
Dynamic Host Configuration Protocol	37
Routing	37
Peering	37
Gateways	38
Load balancers	38
Elastic Load Balancer	38
Application Load Balancer	38
Local traffic manager	39
Intrusion detection and prevention services	39
Shield	39
Web Application Firewall	39
Storage	39
Elastic Block Storage	40
Ephemeral	40
Simple Storage Solution	40
Glacier	40
CloudFront	40
Elastic File System	41
Amazon Machine Images	41
IAM	41
Security Token Service	41
Summary	42
Further reading	43
Chapter 3: Availability Patterns - Understanding Your Needs	45
Technical requirements	45
High availability	46
Top-level domain	46
Regions	50
Load balancing	51
Global Traffic Manager	51
Availability Zones	54
Local Traffic Management	54
Health checks	56
Fault tolerance	57
Auto scaling	57
Placement groups	58

Hierarchical storage management	58
Summary	61
Exercises	61
Further reading	61
Chapter 4: Security - Ensuring the Integrity of Your Systems	**63**
Technical requirements	63
Shared responsibilities	64
Cloud specific	64
Governance	64
Risk	65
Compliance	65
Inheritance	65
Defense in depth	66
Least privilege	66
Users	66
In transit	66
VPC	67
Security groups – port filtering	67
Network ACLs – subnet	68
Obscurity	69
Application	70
At rest	72
Credentials	73
Certificates	74
Keys	74
CloudHSM	75
RBAC	76
Directory service	76
More IAM	76
Users	77
Instance profiles	78
Cognito	79
User pools	79
Identity pools	79
Logging	80
CloudTrail	80
CloudWatch events	81
Flow logs	81
GuardDuty	83
Vulnerability scanning	83
Instance-level scanning	83
Containers	84
Code and functions	84
Buckets	84
Network	84

  Cloud environment   85
Summary   85
Further reading   85

Section 2: DevOps Patterns

Chapter 5: Continuous Deployment - Introducing New Features with Minimal Risk   89
 Technical requirements   90
 Source control   90
 CodeBuild   90
  Projects   96
  Event-driven architecture   100
  Build servers   105
 Testing your code   105
 Summary   110
 Further reading   110

Chapter 6: Ephemeral Environments - Sandboxes for Experiments   111
 Developer productivity   111
 Exploring deployment strategies   112
 Facilitating self-service   113
  Templates   114
 Using multiple environments   115
 Testing your environment   115
 Managing cost   118
 Summary   120
 Exercises   121

Chapter 7: Operation and Maintenance - Keeping Things Running at Peak Performance   123
 Technical requirements   123
 Desilofication   124
  Product mindset   124
  Balanced team   124
  User-centered design   125
  Self-service   125
 Measurement   125
  Indicators   126
  Objectives   126
  Agreements   127
 Fault injection   127
  Reliability testing   127
  Embrace risk   128
 Business continuity   128

Snapshots	128
Restore	130
Disaster recovery	131
Incident response	131
Postmortems	132
Reduction	132
Local development	132
Summary	133
Further reading	133

Chapter 8: Application Virtualization - Using Cloud Native Patterns for Your Workloads — 135

Technical requirements	136
Containers	136
Registry services	138
Elastic Container Service	138
Managed Kubernetes service	139
Serverless	139
Service discovery	147
Summary	148
Further reading	148

Chapter 9: Antipatterns - Avoiding Counterproductive Solutions — 149

Exploring counterproductive processes	149
Lift and shift	150
Change control boards	150
Non-reproducibility	150
Firefighting	151
Can't fail attitude to system uptime	151
Practices to avoid in general	151
Silos	151
Lock in	152
Version control	152
Anti-patterns that you might come across	153
Monoliths	153
Single points of failure	154
Networking	154
Scaling	154
Resilience	155
Summary	156
Further reading	156

Section 3: Persistence Patterns

Chapter 10: Databases - Identifying Which Type Fits Your Needs — 159

General considerations	160

Workflow	160
Vertical versus horizontal scaling	161
Durability—surviving system failure	163
Dimensions	163
Reliability	164
Read versus write	164
Latency	165
Rate of change—static versus dynamic	166
Access frequency—do I ever need this again? Archival for compliance	166
Sizing your storage	167
Streamed	167
Compressed	167
Sparse data	168
Slowly changing data	168
RDS	168
Transactional data	169
CAP Theorem	169
High consistency	170
High availability	170
Partition tolerance	170
Setting up Aurora and MySQL	170
Unstructured data	172
DynamoDB	172
Polyglot persistence	**174**
Text	174
ElasticSearch	174
CloudTrail	176
Elemental MediaStore—dedicated services for video	177
S3 – binary files	178
EMR	179
Graph databases	181
Neptune	181
Time series	183
Timestream	183
Summary	**183**
Further reading	**184**
Chapter 11: Data Processing - Handling Your Data Transformation	**185**
Queuing	**185**
MSK	186
Batching	**187**
Caching	**191**
ElastiCache	191
Event stream processing	**192**
Athena (querying S3)	193
Transforms	**193**
Audio/video (mp4 to mp3)	194

Elastic Transcoder	194
Kinesis	196
CloudTrail	197
Machine learning	199
Amazon SageMaker	199
Jupyter Notebook	201
Amazon Comprehend – NLP	201
AI	202
Anomaly detection	203
Prediction	203
Forecasting	203
Clustering	204
Feature or dimensionality reduction	204
Trees	205
Classification	205
Interpolate missing data (sparsity)	205
Image recognition	206
Pattern recognition	206
Summary	206
Exercises	207
Further reading	207
Chapter 12: Observability - Understanding How Your Products Are Behaving	209
Technical requirements	210
Analyzing your products	210
Logging	210
Metrics	211
CloudWatch	211
Creating metric alarms	212
Viewing available metrics	212
Searching for available metrics	213
Getting statistics for a metric	213
Graphing metrics	215
Publishing custom metrics	216
Using metric math	217
Performance optimization	218
Capacity management	218
AWS dashboards	218
Creating a dashboard	219
Adding or removing a graph	220
Moving or resizing a graph	220
Editing a graph	220
Graphing metrics manually on a CloudWatch dashboard	220
Adding or removing a text widget	221
Adding or removing an alarm	221
Monitoring resources in multiple regions	222
Linking and unlinking graphs	222
Adding a dashboard to your favorites list	222

Changing the time range or time zone format	222
Tracing	**223**
X-Ray	223
Alarms	**223**
Alarm states	**224**
How the alarm state is evaluated when data is missing	225
Events	**226**
Concepts	226
Summary	**228**
Exercises	**228**
Further reading	**229**
Chapter 13: Anti-Patterns - Bypassing Inferior Options	**231**
Building processes	**231**
Analysis paralysis	232
Trash	233
Best practices	**235**
Tight coupling	235
Lock-in	236
Everything is a nail	237
Different patterns	**237**
Polyglot persistence	238
Athena	238
Amazon Simple Queue Service (SQS)	239
DocumentDB	239
DynamoDB	240
ElastiCache	240
Redshift	241
Logging	243
Summarized metrics	245
Summary	**245**
Further reading	**245**
Other Books You May Enjoy	**247**
Index	**251**

Preface

The *Implementing Cloud Design Patterns for AWS* provides reproducible processes, practices, and blueprints to deliver secure, extensible, cloud-native products. This second edition guide will help you leverage the extensive offerings of AWS to solve common problems with it.

You will be introduced to cloud service patterns and discover how to apply them when building microservice-oriented solutions and highly robust systems using the cloud infrastructure. You will begin by creating core components and discern how to add layers of scalable services that can be applied to your products' needs. You will also learn how to leverage container and serverless architectures to increase extensibility and security, thereby exploring and applying Amazon-provided services in unique ways to solve common design problems.

Who this book is for

If you're an architect, solution provider, or DevOps community member looking to implement repeatable patterns to deploy and maintain services in the Amazon cloud infrastructure, this book is for you.

What this book covers

Chapter 1, *Introduction to Amazon Web Services*, briefly introduces you to AWS, where you will not only learn about the background and industry shift that started the movement into utility computing, but also where AWS fits into it.

Chapter 2, *Core Services – Building Blocks for Your Product*, introduces you to various AWS components that you will use to build your products.

Chapter 3, *Availability Patterns – Understanding Your Needs*, combines some of the components into architectures aimed toward creating your own highly available services.

Chapter 4, *Security – Ensuring the Integrity of Your Systems*, covers some of the best security practices that will allow you to establish a perimeter around all of your products from the start.

Preface

Chapter 5, *Continuous Deployment – Introducing New Features with Minimal Risk*, covers some of the practices that you can use to provide a continuous deployment pipeline, which will enable you to put your product in front of your clients quickly and in a reliable and reproducible way, whether this includes new product features, experiments, or configurations.

Chapter 6, *Ephemeral Environments – Sandboxes for Experiments*, supplies a design pattern to aid you in your move to the cloud. The financial benefits, the advantages for your customers, and the improved velocity of your software engineers will be considered. Some high-level topics that are making headlines in the DevOps movement and can improve our productivity within AWS will also be covered.

Chapter 7, *Operation and Maintenance – Keeping Things Running at Peak Performance*, combines various processes that will help you to deliver a product with high availability and ensure that, in the event of a disaster, you have practiced your recovery methods.

Chapter 8, *Application Virtualization – Using Cloud Native Patterns for Your Workloads*, shows how to isolate services for performance improvements and cost savings. You will inspect the choices available for reducing product complexity and review enterprise patterns for mitigating failures through the separation of concerns

Chapter 9, *Antipatterns – Avoiding Counterproductive Solutions*, attends to the difficulties you might encounter as your product complexity grows.

Chapter 10, *Databases – Identifying Which Type Fits Your Needs*, helps identify how to collect and learn from data that can help you avoid anomalies that haven't been widely encountered in the cloud yet.

Chapter 11, *Data Processing – Handling Your Data Transformation*, discusses various techniques for processing the data in your infrastructure, especially in the field of machine learning.

Chapter 12, *Observability – Understanding How Your Products Are Behaving*, covers how to observe your application with logging, metrics, and tracing, which will help you track changes in your infrastructure, find inconsistencies, and provide insights into process improvements.

Chapter 13, *Anti-Patterns – Bypassing Inferior Options*, analyzes persistence paradigms, that are ineffective and may result in undesired consequences.

To get the most out of this book

You'll need prior experience of using AWS to be able to understand the key concepts covered in the book, as it focuses on the patterns rather than the basics of using AWS.

Download the example code files

You can download the example code files for this book from your account at `www.packt.com`. If you purchased this book elsewhere, you can visit `www.packt.com/support` and register to have the files emailed directly to you.

You can download the code files by following these steps:

1. Log in or register at `www.packt.com`.
2. Select the **SUPPORT** tab.
3. Click on **Code Downloads & Errata**.
4. Enter the name of the book in the **Search** box and follow the onscreen instructions.

Once the file is downloaded, please make sure that you unzip or extract the folder using the latest version of the following:

- WinRAR/7-Zip for Windows
- Zipeg/iZip/UnRarX for Mac
- 7-Zip/PeaZip for Linux

The code bundle for the book is also hosted on GitHub at `https://github.com/PacktPublishing/Implementing-Cloud-Design-Patterns-for-AWS-Second-Edition`. In case there's an update to the code, it will be updated on the existing GitHub repository.

We also have other code bundles from our rich catalog of books and videos available at `https://github.com/PacktPublishing/`. Check them out!

Conventions used

There are a number of text conventions used throughout this book.

`CodeInText`: Indicates code words in text, database table names, folder names, filenames, file extensions, pathnames, dummy URLs, user input, and Twitter handles. Here is an example: "Save the file in your `ch2` folder as `terraform_install.sh`."

A block of code is set as follows:

```
provider "aws" {
region = "us-east-1"
}
resource "aws_codecommit_repository" "cloudpatterns" {
repository_name = "cloudpatternsrepo"
description = "This is a demonstration repository for the AWS Cloud Patterns book."
}
```

When we wish to draw your attention to a particular part of a code block, the relevant lines or items are set in bold:

```
provider "aws" {
region = "us-east-1"
}
resource "aws_codecommit_repository" "cloudpatterns" {
repository_name = "cloudpatternsrepo"
description = "This is a demonstration repository for the AWS Cloud Patterns book."
}
```

Any command-line input or output is written as follows:

```
git config --global credential.UseHttpPath true
git init
```

Bold: Indicates a new term, an important word, or words that you see onscreen. For example, words in menus or dialog boxes appear in the text like this. Here is an example: "You can close the **Run** window."

Warnings or important notes appear like this.

Tips and tricks appear like this.

Get in touch

Feedback from our readers is always welcome.

General feedback: If you have questions about any aspect of this book, mention the book title in the subject of your message and email us at customercare@packtpub.com.

Errata: Although we have taken every care to ensure the accuracy of our content, mistakes do happen. If you have found a mistake in this book, we would be grateful if you would report this to us. Please visit www.packt.com/submit-errata, selecting your book, clicking on the Errata Submission Form link, and entering the details.

Piracy: If you come across any illegal copies of our works in any form on the Internet, we would be grateful if you would provide us with the location address or website name. Please contact us at copyright@packt.com with a link to the material.

If you are interested in becoming an author: If there is a topic that you have expertise in and you are interested in either writing or contributing to a book, please visit authors.packtpub.com.

Reviews

Please leave a review. Once you have read and used this book, why not leave a review on the site that you purchased it from? Potential readers can then see and use your unbiased opinion to make purchase decisions, we at Packt can understand what you think about our products, and our authors can see your feedback on their book. Thank you!

For more information about Packt, please visit packt.com.

Section 1: The Basics

In this section, you will become familiar with the building blocks available from AWS. You will also learn how to create a cheap, scalable, and secure solution for your business.

The following chapters are included in this section:

- `Chapter 1`, *Introduction to Amazon Web Services*
- `Chapter 2`, *Core Services – Building Blocks for Your Product*
- `Chapter 3`, *Availability Patterns – Understanding Your Needs*
- `Chapter 4`, *Security – Ensuring the Integrity of Your Systems*

Introduction to Amazon Web Services

Welcome to the first chapter of this book, *Implementing Cloud Design Patterns for AWS, Second Edition*. After a brief history of the development of the cloud and the part that AWS plays in it, we'll look into the Amazon philosophy. An exploration of some of its most well-known customers will give us a platform to dive into the reasons why it's a good choice for your product development effort. We'll survey the service offerings from AWS and create a trial account, which you can use to develop your products.

This chapter will briefly cover the following topics:

- Introduction to AWS
- Utility computing
- Categories of service offerings
- Benefits of moving to the cloud

Introduction to AWS

Amazon—aren't they an online bookstore? This is what someone in the late 1990s might have asked. Nowadays, with nearly 40% of the e-commerce market in the US and over 30% in India, everyone knows who they are. But not so well-known outside of technology circles is **Amazon Web Services (AWS)**. Amazon describes this part of the business as follows:

> *AWS is a secure cloud services platform* (https://aws.amazon.com/what-is-cloud-computing/), *offering compute power, database storage, content delivery, and other functionality to help businesses scale and grow. Millions of customers* (https://aws.amazon.com/solutions/case-studies/) *are currently leveraging AWS cloud products* (https://aws.amazon.com/products/) *and solutions* (https://aws.amazon.com/solutions/) *to build sophisticated applications with increased flexibility, scalability, and reliability* (https://aws.amazon.com/what-is-aws/).

Amazon is currently the leader in the cloud infrastructure business with 33% market share—about the same as Google Cloud, Azure, and IBM combined. They're using their huge lead, and the profits from it, to invest in new services to further differentiate themselves. Since the publishing of the first edition of this book, they've added hundreds of new offerings. Millions of customers are taking advantage of these services. The initial target market of startups and small businesses has spawned web-scale enterprises such as Netflix, Pinterest, and Airbnb. The Fortune 500 and governments around the world are also on board.

On an annual basis, all of Amazon's operating income derived from AWS in 2017 (https://www.zdnet.com/article/all-of-amazons-2017-operating-income-comes-from-aws/).

History

How we got here provides valuable lessons for building your product and scaling it globally. The retail business is peaky. Amazon needed capacity to meet its highest demand period during Thanksgiving and Black Friday. Come January, it had a whole lot of hardware sitting around, underutilized. Having worked for years providing e-commerce services to partners, they were able to take their internal offerings and make them available to the public. Utility computing was born.

This pattern has been repeated many times. Amazon is constantly adding services to tackle new and unique problems that they have encountered within their own business. Those internal services then get previewed and customer feedback is collected. When they meet a certain service level, they're released for use by anyone with a credit card. You need to use this same strategy for your products.

The future

Product-driven development will continue to evolve within the Amazon ecosystem. The benefits that are identified internally will trickle down to all of the AWS cloud users. Newer services will continue to simplify the consumption of complex offerings. Economics of scale will push prices lower while moving resources closer to your customers.

Product

Whether you're developing new features for Amazon or your local football club, or hoping to create the next Netflix, you need to be focused on your product. The patterns in this book have helped people develop and scale their products. Throughout this book, we'll build **Minimum Viable Products (MVP)** (`http://www.startuplessonslearned.com/2009/08/minimum-viable-product-guide.html`) on AWS.

Amazon will continue to use this pattern to develop new services, and you should too.

Data

The third part of this book looks at persistence. The item we are persisting is data. AWS offers a number of services to help us manage the volume, velocity, and variety of data. Other products will help identify the veracity and value in the flood. In `Chapter 11`, *Data Processing - Handling Your Data Transformation*, we'll use another set of tools to predict how our customers are going to react to new features. Continuous experimentation and measurement allow our product to become more successful.

Code

AWS also provides a number of open source projects as services (https://www.slideshare.net/AmazonWebServices/aws-reinvent-2016-open-source-at-awscontributions-support-and-engagementarc213). This allows them to leverage large active communities for product development and bug hunting. In the case of the AWS Software Development Kit for Python, Boto (https://github.com/boto/boto3), Amazon has taken over the project. We're not going to go into all of the benefits of open source here, but remember that many of the services included in our patterns are available as source code to everyone.

Coding is going to be an important part of your product, the systems that run it, and the people that use it. We'll be writing code to allow the reuse and modification of our cloud patterns. To get into the spirit of things, we'll be using a cloud-based development tool that was originally written by the open source Mozilla foundation. A group of the developers decided to create a freemium model to provide support for people using their **Integrated Development Environment (IDE)**, Cloud9. Amazon bought the company—another great pattern for applying to your product.

Utility computing

The cloud is an extension of the practice of co-locating hardware at a site away from your company. Historically, you would put your stuff closer to a fast connection in order to get your pages to load more quickly. Amazon stretched the market by allowing you to run your product on their hardware. They further innovated by creating a utility model that lets you pay for only what you need.

Anything as a Service

Obviously, IDE as a service was not the first service offering of AWS, but it fit well with their philosophy of **Anything as a Service** (often abbreviated as **XaaS**). By going beyond their initial offering of co-located virtual machines, Amazon has redefined existing infrastructure services. Providing configurable services and software implementations of hardware found in data centers has allowed them to develop complementary products such as load balancing, content delivery networks, and security plus, failover and replication solutions. Extending their internal tools or purchasing synergistic products such as Cloud9 has provided the full stack developer an opportunity to use a well thought out, low cost, pay for use, integrated suite.

AWS provides three primary categories of service offerings:

- **Infrastructure as a Service (IaaS)**
- **Platform as a Service (PaaS)**
- **Software as a Service (SaaS)**

Infrastructure as a Service

IaaS can be described as a service that provides virtual abstractions for hardware, servers, and networking components. The service provider owns all of the equipment and is responsible for its housing, running, and maintenance. In this case, AWS provides **Application Programming Interfaces (APIs)**, SDKs, and a web console for creating and modifying virtual machines; their network components; routers; gateways; subnets; load balancers; and much more. Where a user with a physical data center would incur charges for the hardware, power, and connectivity, this is removed by IaaS with a payment model that's per-hour (or per-use). Specific IaaS components will be the building blocks for our product. A discussion of the key pieces will take place in `Chapter 2`, *Core Services - Building Blocks for Your Product*.

Platform as a Service

While AWS doesn't provide a full-blown PaaS offering such as Cloud Foundry (`https://www.cloudfoundry.org/`) at the moment, it has a number of products that can simplify the product development experience. Its broad service catalog can also be used to compose a DIY platform. PaaS is described as the delivery of a computing platform, typically an operating system, programming language execution environment, database, or web server. With AWS, a user can easily turn a code base into a running environment without having to worry about any of the pieces underneath, such as setting up and maintaining the database, web server, or code runtime versions. It also allows your product to be scaled without having to do anything other than set policies through the configuration. We'll survey the services for on-demand expansion in `Chapter 3`, *Availability Patterns - Understanding Your Needs*.

Software as a Service

The best interpretation for the SaaS model is on-demand software. The user need only configure the software to use and interact with it. The draw to SaaS is that there's no need to learn how to deploy the software to get it working in a larger stack, and generally the charges are per-usage-hour. In the case of AWS, much of the maintenance burden is also removed.

The AWS suite is both impressive and unique in that it doesn't fall under any one of the cloud service models we described previously. Until AWS made its name, the need to virtualize an entire environment or stack was usually not an easy task and required integration of different providers offerings, each solving a specific part of the deployment puzzle. The cost of using many different providers to create a virtual stack might not be cheaper than the initial hardware cost for moving equipment into a data center. Besides the cost of the providers themselves, having multiple providers also created the problem of scaling in one area and notifying another of the changes. While making applications more resilient and scalable, this Frankenstein method usually did not simplify the problem as a whole.

Cloud continuum

When you build your first MVP for venture capitalists or an internal review board, we recommend you do it fast and focus on the user experience. In most cases, the monolith you create isn't going to be able to achieve web scale. The Cloud-Native Maturity Model is based on the twelve factor design principals. Its focus is on how to run your applications on the cloud: `https://pivotal.io/replatforming`

AWS supplies all of the services that are needed to launch cloud-native applications. We'll start with a cloud-friendly product, then in `Chapter 8`, *Application Virtualization - Using Cloud Native Patterns for Your Workloads*, we'll go into great depth. First, let's look at some of the trends driving cloud adoption.

Microservices

In most cases, the monolith you create is not going to be able to achieve web scale. As you break off pieces to refactor, you'll develop smaller services. This allows for the decoupling of components upgrade schedules, which speeds up product development. By adopting the continuous delivery pattern espoused by Jez Humble, you can deploy new features and measure their success quickly. We'll take a peek at these architectures in `Chapter 5`, *Continuous Deployment - Introducing New Features with Minimal Risk*. Isolation of your microservices will be the subject of `Chapter 4`, *Security - Ensuring the Integrity of Your Systems*.

By providing easy to use, low cost SaaS options, AWS lets you focus on building software. High value feature development replaces low level toil. In `Chapter 6`, *Ephemeral Environments - Sandboxes for Experiments*, we'll present patterns that help foster collaboration between developers and operators. AWS composable services empower all team members to participate in the product development they know best.

Crazy new services

Amazon has introduced thousands of services since the introduction of the **Elastic Cloud Compute** (**EC2**), their first publicly available multi-tenant virtualization offering.

Hardware virtualization or platform virtualization refers to the creation of a virtual machine (`https://en.wikipedia.org/wiki/Virtual_machine`) that acts like a real computer with an operating system.

Most of them are enhancements to their MVP. Many of the services are tucked away in the management console. All of them are constantly monitored to ensure that customers are happy and to identify opportunities for new features. The container and serverless patterns in `Chapter 8`, *Application Virtualization - Using Cloud Native Patterns for Your Workloads*, promote self-contained service development for your product. Some, such as the **Internet of Things** (**IoT**) services, are out of scope for this book.

Free trials

If you don't have an AWS account, you can sign up for a free one at https://aws.amazon.com:

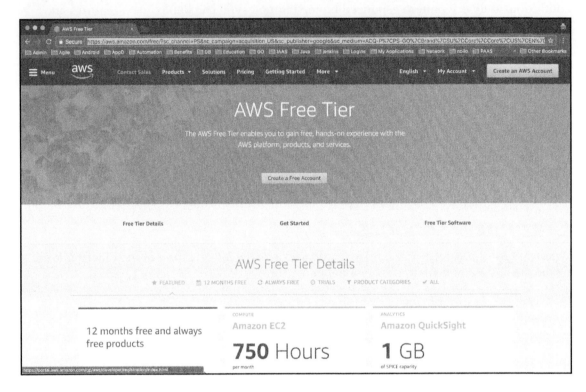

Chapter 1

You'll need a valid email, phone number, and credit card (in case you go over your allotted capacity):

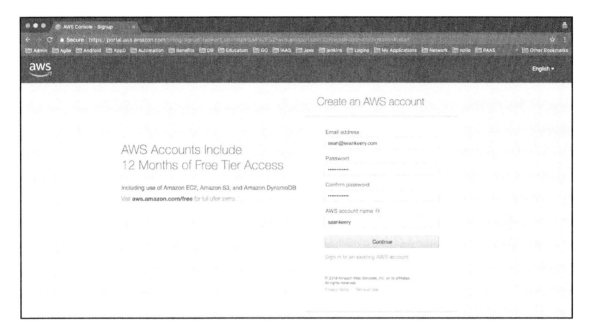

The exercises in this book will use many of the free AWS services. We'll note when there are pay-per-use services that may be a better solution for certain classes of problems.

Huge catalog

AWS learned from the Amazon e-commerce team the value of partnerships. Just like you can shop the Crocs store on the parent side, you can rent an in-memory data grid powered by Apache Geode for a few hours through the AWS marketplace. The AWS marketplace provides an avenue where users can purchase or trial third-party images that provide configurable services such as databases and web applications. As a product developer, you can easily add your offerings to the exchange:

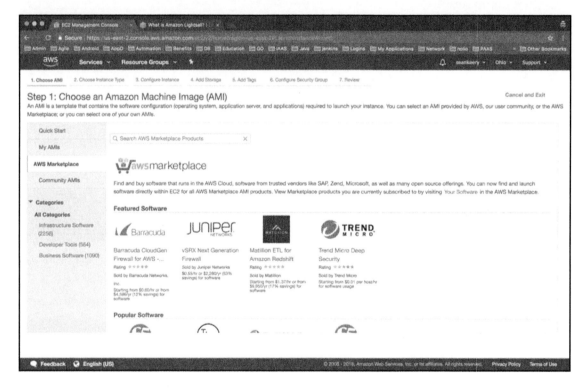

In the spirit of competition, a lot of the software in the marketplace offers competition to the AWS native services. Operations engineers may find it easier to move workloads to the cloud by reusing components that they're familiar with, such as F5 load balancers, instead of the AWS Elastic Load Balancers (Chapter 2, *Core Services - Building Blocks for Your Product*). Other products, such as the trend Micro Deep Security Agent, fill in gaps where AWS doesn't currently have a solution. Partnerships with Microsoft, VMware, and Tableau let you easily migrate internal workloads or extend your data center to the cloud.

Software defined, API driven

The adoption of a DevOps culture for your product team provides you with similar cooperation benefits. Getting operations engineers involved in product development helps eliminate hand-offs. Developers being on call for production issues acquaints them with troubleshooting practices and boosts empathy for users. By working together, the product team can establish a clear contact for use. Well-defined APIs are an excellent way to ensure that the contract can be met. AWS publishes extensive documentation for its interfaces, as well as defining service-level objectives for its products.

Benefits of moving to the cloud

For a new product, you should start development in the cloud to take advantage of Amazon's well-thought-out offerings. For existing companies, the AWS suite can handle almost everything a modern data center can while significantly reducing your operating costs. The shift suits small teams but, for mid-sized teams, the effort that's saved begins to outweigh the cost. In larger organizations, AWS can also help you get rid of some of the process bottlenecks that come with a data center. Requesting, provisioning, repairs, and scheduling downtime are all streamlined. There are many different answers to why moving to the cloud might be beneficial. We'll start at mid-sized because this is the size that usually includes the two teams that benefit the most. Let's take a look at our personas:

- The software engineer
- The operations engineer
- The product owner

Software engineer

For a software developer, the ability to share code and delivery tools across teams is critical. AWS gives you the ability to enforce consistency across environments. Different versions of core languages or libraries can be avoided by having uniform templates. Chapter 5, *Continuous Deployment - Introducing New Features with Minimal Risk*, emphasizes how these good continuous delivery practices in the cloud can lower business risk. Chapter 3, *Availability Patterns - Understanding Your Needs*, goes deeper on making sure your product is available, while Chapter 4, *Security - Ensuring the Integrity of Your Systems*, covers how a secure groundwork can be inherited across products and services. We'll lay out how developers can easily build cost-effective products, which can grow as demand intensifies. Data management patterns in Chapter 10, *Databases - Identifying which Type Fits Your Needs*, and Chapter 11, *Data Processing - Handling Your Data Transformation*, will help software engineers understand the trade-offs in architecting their MVPs.

Introduction to Amazon Web Services

The ability to spin up entire environments for testing and simulation in AWS is amazing. Providing developers with their own sandboxes improves their ability to innovate and deliver new features at a high velocity. In the cloud-native world, a single environment can be encapsulated on a single EC2 instance. We'll explore how application virtualization can further improve developer productivity in Chapter 8, *Application Virtualization - Using Cloud Native Patterns for Your Workloads*.

Operations engineer

Throwaway environments are also be beneficial to the operations teams. In Chapter 6, *Ephemeral Environments - Sandboxes for Experiments*, we'll show you how to take centralized configuration, which describes AWS resources, map them into a dependency graph, and create an entire stack. This flexibility would be nearly impossible in traditional hardware settings and provides an on-demand mentality—not just for the base application, but also for the entire infrastructure, leading to a more agile core.

The operations team's responsibility differs greatly from company to company, but it's safe to assume that the team is heavily involved with monitoring the applications and systems for issues and possible optimizations. AWS provides enough infrastructure for monitoring and acting on metrics, and an entire book could be dedicated to the topic. For an operations team, the benefit of moving to Amazon might justify itself only to alleviate all of the work involved in duplicating this functionality elsewhere, allowing the team to focus on creating deeper and more meaningful system health checks. There will be more coverage of operations in Chapter 7, *Operation and Maintenance - Keeping Things Running at Peak Performance*, while observability will be addressed in Chapter 12, *Observability - Understanding How Your Products Are Behaving*.

Product owner

As a product owner, the low cost of entry into very complex technology is a huge win. Chapter 3, *Availability Patterns - Understanding Your Needs*, will analyze the cost benefits of using AWS to provide global availability. The ability to move from hourly pricing to longer term subscriptions will give you a good baseline for product operating expenses. Avoiding inferior and counterproductive solutions will be the topic of Chapter 9, *Antipatterns - Avoiding Counterproductive Solutions*, and Chapter 13, *Anti-Patterns - Bypassing Inferior Options*. The shared responsibility model AWS provides will be explored in Chapter 4, *Security - Ensuring the Integrity of Your Systems*. By inheriting industry standard security controls, you can concentrate on user-centric product aspects.

Letting AWS manage the services at scale lets you avoid investing in dedicated support staff. Amazon has also adopted the freemium pattern for their own support. Start small and expand if you need more help:

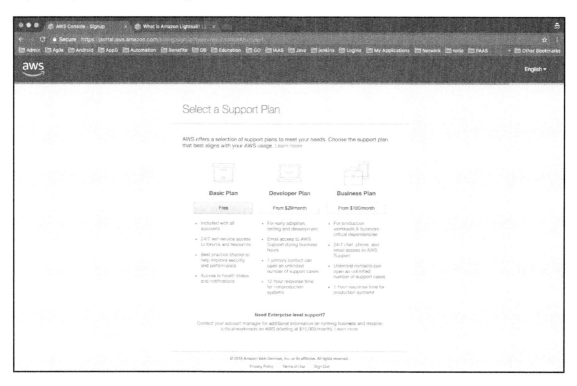

Summary

Throughout this brief introduction to AWS, we learned not only about the background and industry shift that started the movement into utility computing, but also where AWS fits into it. We touched on the kinds of problems AWS can solve and where its services are competitive. There are countless unique processes to be solved with this ever-growing environment. Picking up consistent patterns throughout this book will help you strengthen products of many forms and protect against risk. In the following chapters, we'll go over some of the core services that are used to create basic design patterns. These patterns will be used to deliver more complex architectures using DevOps and data best practices in the *DevOps Patterns* and *Persistence Patterns* sections.

Further reading

A crash course in virtualization is available here: `https://www.packtpub.com/application-development/introduction-virtualization-one-hour-crash-course-video`.

An in-depth overview of the different cloud service models can be found in the following video: `https://www.packtpub.com/virtualization-and-cloud/learn-cloud-computing-scratch-video`.

2
Core Services - Building Blocks for Your Product

In this chapter, we will look at the components available for you to use. Whether you are a traditional software engineer, a DevOps practitioner, or a systems administrator, you need to use practices that allow the creation, and re-creation, of consistent, extensible, and portable products. Amazon's **application programming interface** (**API**) driven services simplify mixing these services in order to synthesize new products. We will explore how we can apply patterns from successful projects while improving our capacity to add features with limited exposure. All of our patterns will be based on code. Using this code, we will build a skeleton for web-scale operations. A model containing processing, storage, networking, and security will become the backbone for future product improvements. If you are already familiar with the AWS components, skip this chapter, or skip to `Chapter 3`, *Availability Patterns - Understanding Your Needs*.

The following topics will be covered in brief:

- Code
- Compute
- Networking
- Storage
- **Identity and Access Management (IAM)**

Technical requirements

All of the development in this book has been done using the Chrome browser on OSX. Open source tools will be used to fill any gaps in the AWS ecosystem. We will be using Git (https://github.com/git/git) for version control of our source control. No install is required, as it is built into the cloud-based tool we will use for our development. Our configuration management will be done using Terraform (https://www.terraform.io/). Installation will take place once we have our development environment set up.

The code for this chapter can be found at: https://github.com/PacktPublishing/Implementing-Cloud-Design-Patterns-for-AWS-Second-Edition/tree/master/Chapter02.

Code

Everything as code is going to be our mantra. Some code will be declarative, for systems automation. Other code will be procedural, having an easily understood flow. Functions will be used in some cases, and objects in others. We will need places to write this code, keep this code, build artifacts from it, then deploy it. Our building blocks will rely on Terraform and we will install that software later in this chapter. We're using Terraform to define our environments because it is becoming a de facto standard—it's fairly easy to pick up, it's capable of targeting multiple cloud providers, and it's open source. We're not going to look at the Terraform resources (code) for all of the AWS components in this chapter, but as we build solutions in later chapters, we'll come across a lot of them.

Cloud9

Although we said everything is going to be code, and while it is possible to create our **integrated development environment** (**IDE**) as code, we are going to use the AWS console for this exercise. Log in to the console, click the **Services** button, and search or scroll to the Cloud9 service. This cloud native IDE is provided for us by Amazon, so we will use it in order to simplify our security and easily integrate with other AWS services. Go ahead and create an environment (press the big orange **Create environment** button):

Chapter 2

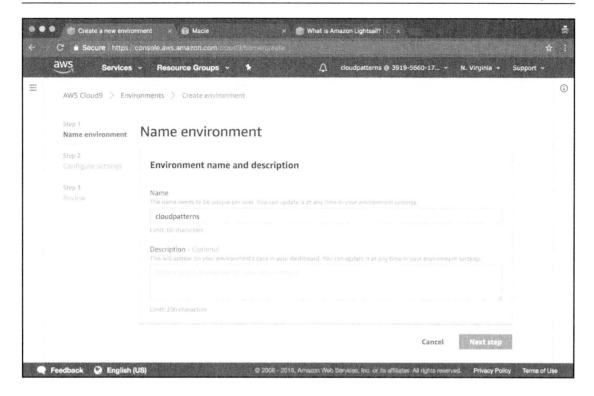

If, when you access services, you receive a warning on the page about being logged in as a root user, you should consider adding in a less privileged user through the IAM service. IAM is covered later in this chapter.

Select the smallest available option (when we were writing this book, it was the **t2.micro (1 GiB RAM + 1 vCPU)** instance type) for now and keep all of the other defaults. Press the button at the bottom of the page for the **Next step**:

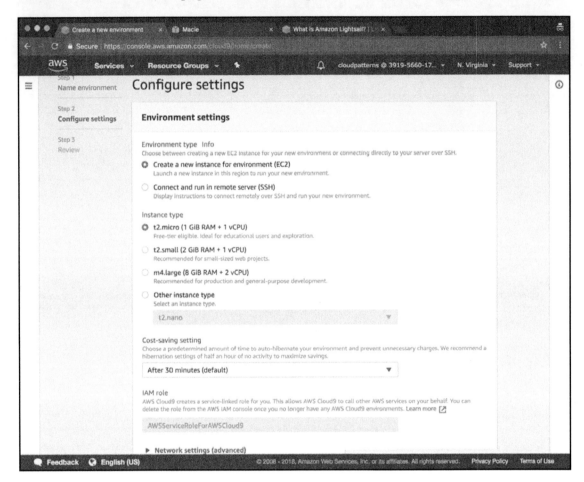

Check the settings on the **Review** step page and confirm; you should then eventually see something like the following screenshot. Creating environments takes a few minutes:

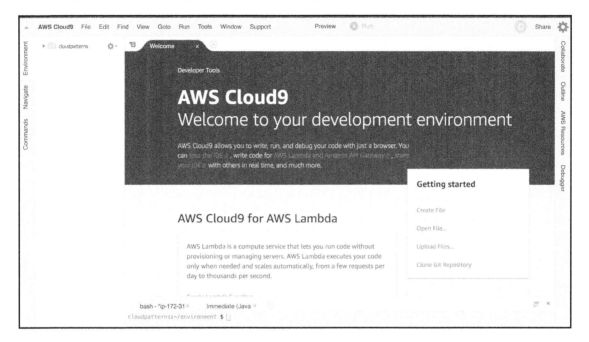

Core Services - Building Blocks for Your Product

Right-click on the `cloudpatterns` folder and create a new folder called `ch2`:

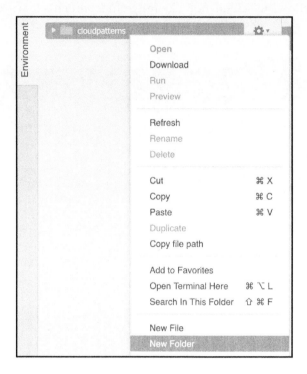

Now we will install Terraform to help us to manage our infrastructure as code configuration. Click **Create File** and add the following code:

```
#! /bin/bash
mkdir download
cd download/
wget
https://releases.hashicorp.com/terraform/0.11.11/terraform_0.11.11_linux_amd64.zip
unzip terraform_0.11.11_linux_amd64.zip
mv terraform /usr/bin/terraform
terraform
exit
```

 HashiCorp releases new Terraform versions frequently. Use the latest version on the download page (https://www.terraform.io/downloads.html) as it will contain bug fixes, new features, and security patches.

Chapter 2

 If you find that this script fails, the most likely reason is that you're using an IAM user. You will need to prepend lines 6 and 7 with `sudo` to make this work.

Save the file in your `ch2` folder as `terraform_install.sh`, then click **Run**:

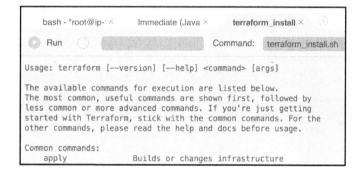

You will see some scrolling at the bottom of your window, then Terraform help will appear. You can close the **Run** window and click in the bash window:

Now that we have some source code, we need a place to keep it outside of Cloud9. We will create an AWS CodeCommit source repository using Terraform. Let's start with a new `codecommit.tf` file:

```
provider "aws" {
 region = "us-east-1"
}
resource "aws_codecommit_repository" "cloudpatterns" {
  repository_name = "cloudpatternsrepo"
  description = "This is a demonstration repository for the AWS Cloud Patterns book."
}
```

[29]

Core Services - Building Blocks for Your Product

 I'm going to use spaces to indent my code. Some people use tabs.

We need to initialize the Terraform environment using `terraform init` first. This will configure the AWS provider for you. Then, you can run `terraform apply`:

```
bash - "root@ip-    Immediate (Java

cloudpatterns:~/environment $ terraform apply
data.aws_codecommit_repository.cloudpatterns: Refreshing state...

Apply complete! Resources: 0 added, 0 changed, 0 destroyed.
cloudpatterns:~/environment $ terraform show
data.aws_codecommit_repository.cloudpatterns:
  id = cloudpatternsrepo
  arn = arn:aws:codecommit:us-east-1:391956601792:cloudpatternsrepo
  clone_url_http = https://git-codecommit.us-east-1.amazonaws.com/v1/repos/cloudpatternsrepo
  clone_url_ssh = ssh://git-codecommit.us-east-1.amazonaws.com/v1/repos/cloudpatternsrepo
  repository_id = 3e8a86d6-605a-44b0-b2ab-2c55f27e2c7b
  repository_name = cloudpatternsrepo

cloudpatterns:~/environment $
```

Great! Let's put our code into our repository.

 You could have also used the built-in AWS CLI to create your repository from your bash window. The command would have been: `aws codecommit create-repository --repository-name cloudpatternsrepo --repository-description "This is a demonstration repository for the AWS Cloud Patterns book." --region us-east-1`.

Here is some example code for creating a Cloud9 environment with Terraform, `create_env.tf`:

```
resource "aws_cloud9_environment_ec2" "cloudpatterns" {
  instance_type = "t2.micro"
  name = "example-env"
  automatic_stop_time_minutes = "30"
  description = "My Cloud Patterns Environment"
}
```

Some of the code in this book is adapted from the AWS Terraform provider documentation under the Mozilla Public License 2.0. It is available at https://github.com/terraform-providers/terraform-provider-aws/.

CodeCommit

CodeCommit gives you private GitHub repositories. To connect the preceding repository you created, copy the URL or click on the **Clone URL** button as shown in the following screenshot:

Add the repository by running the following commands in the bash panel:

```
git config --global credential.helper '!aws codecommit credential-helper $@'
git config --global credential.UseHttpPath true
git init
git clone git config --global credential.helper '!aws codecommit credential-helper $@'
git remote add
https://git-codecommit.us-east-1.amazonaws.com/v1/repos/cloudpatternsrepo
```

Add and commit your files using the following commands:

```
git add create_env.tf
git commit -am 'terraform example file using instance credentials'
git push
```

Now, you can see them in CodeCommit:

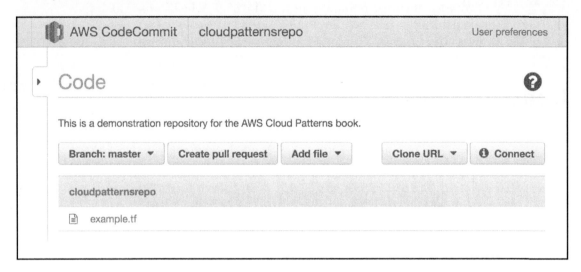

As we move to more complex workflows, we will be using CodeBuild to compile our code. Our continuous delivery model requires a deployment mechanism for updating product features when they are complete. CodeDeploy lets us do this in an automated, repeatable fashion while helping us to avoid typing mistakes.

AWS also provides template repositories in its CodeStar service. These frameworks give you an excellent starting point for web services.

Compute

AWS supports numerous compute models. The highest level, allowing for the most customization, is the instance. **Elastic Cloud Compute (EC2)** is the name of the AWS instance product. The instance is equivalent to a virtual machine run by ESX or KVM in your own data center. The container is available in the **Elastic Container Service (ECS)** or through **Elastic Kubernetes Service (EKS)**. Containers are used for process isolation and increasing utilization density on your physical hardware. Lambda is an offering where the software function is the unit of processing.

Instances

EC2 is the instance level service offering. We already created an instance when we spun up our Cloud9 environment. Using Terraform, we can create another one very easily. Create the following `example.tf` file:

```
resource "aws_instance" "example" {
  ami = "ami-2757f631"
  instance_type = "t2.micro"
}
output "id" {
  value = "${aws_instance.example.id}"
}
```

Run `terraform apply`. The output will be kept in your state file for future use:

```
cloudpatterns:~/environment/cloudpatternsrepo (master) $ terraform output
id = i-09d05d69c4b7f390b
```

We can easily destroy it with `terraform destroy`. If you like, you can try it now. Bringing the environments back is as simple as running `terraform apply`.

One thing to note about `terraform destroy` is that it can be unreliable in practice, especially if the environment is quite complicated. It pays to check that everything has been torn down successfully after the command has completed.

Types

You can get different processor and memory configurations on your instances. Let's abstract our provider into a root file and move our outputs into a file of their own called `main.tf`:

```
provider "aws" {
  region = "us-east-1"
}
module "compute" {
  source = "./compute"
}
```

And we will do the same for another file called `outputs.tf`:

```
output "id" {
  value = "${aws_instance.example.id}"
}
```

And finally, we can do this for the `variables.tf` file:

```
variable "zones" {
  default = ["us-east-1a", "us-east-1b"]
}
```

Usage

In the following sections, we briefly cover the different types of instances that are available with AWS. The types available are shared, dedicated, and spot. These instance types vary in availability, as explained.

Shared

The original AWS compute type was a shared instance. It is the default and usually cheapest option available. Shared instances are the basis for the cloud. It allows Amazon to oversubscribe its hardware. Many people can actually be leveraging the same physical hardware at the same time without using all of its capacity. The term *utility computing* comes from the consumer not really caring what machine they are running on, as long as their instances are running.

Dedicated

As your workloads grow in size, or for regulatory reasons, you may need to separate your compute from other AWS customers. In this case, you would choose a dedicated instance. The dedicated type provides you with your own hardware. It helps to avoid noisy neighbors and simplifies compliance. As you are preventing Amazon from taking advantage of any unused capacity, it has a higher cost.

Spot or ephemeral

Spot instances are the lowest cost CPU capacity available. As the name implies, these instances can disappear at any time. Amazon will give you a two-minute warning to evacuate your workload. For non-critical, resumable workloads, these are an excellent choice.

Raw

For more mature development organizations, AWS offers further virtualization options. These higher level abstractions remove some of the cost associated with instances. We'll jump into more detail about how to take advantage of containers and serverless components in the *DevOps Patterns* section. For now, let's take a look at which parts of the traditional deployment stack/environment we can replace by taking advantage of the offerings provided by AWS.

Containers

AWS has two distinct container-based offerings. Amazon ECS offers a Docker orchestration service while EKS uses Kubernetes as its management plane. Both services share common runtime and packaging components, so you can develop for one and switch to the other painlessly. In both cases, the container image should contain just a minimal operating system and a single application. This practice helps to enforce separation of concerns, simplifies testing, encourages sharing, and allows for easy deployment. Throughout this book, we will use containers to reduce cost and enforce security.

Functions

Lambda is the name of the function-as-a-service or serverless product on AWS. The primary unit of deployment is the function. Lambda supports a large number of programming languages and ingress methods. It leverages containers behind the scenes to very quickly start up on-demand processes. Because these processes are not allowed to run for very long, Amazon can run a lot of them on their infrastructure. This allows them to charge by the millisecond. Coordinating thousands of different functions can be very challenging and we'll stick with simple examples in upcoming chapters.

Networking

Once we have our compute running, we need our instances to talk to each other or our customers. AWS provides very sophisticated options to ensure that communications are fast, reliable, secure, and easy to configure.

Internet Protocol

The basis for the internet and all cloud computing is the **Internet Protocol** (**IP**). All IP addresses are currently using the IPv4 standard. By default, any addresses you create are not available publicly outside of your account.

Elastic IP

AWS has a pool of public IP addresses that can be used by their customers. You are billed for an **Elastic IP** (**EIP**) if you don't have it attached to an instance. This is because the IPv4 address space is almost completely used.

IPv6

The newest version of the IP standard is v6. Current allocations provide for 4,000 addresses for every person on the planet. You must explicitly opt-in to using it on AWS, and it is not available for all services yet.

Route 53

To hide the complexity of the IP address space, we will use the **Domain Name Service** (**DNS**). Amazon's implementation of DNS is called **Route 53**. In addition to standard services, AWS adds some very valuable features.

DNS

Amazon allows you to manage your own domains (such as `book.seankeery.com`) programmatically. AWS also acts as a registrar, letting you create new domains with ease. Domain delegation provides a mechanism for hosting part of your DNS at Amazon as you migrate to the cloud.

Global traffic manager

Beyond the standard DNS services, AWS lets you add sophisticated load balancing features to your services. You can configure DNS to take advantage of distributed instances. Route 53 can also be used to distribute requests based on how close your customers are to a service. Finally, Route 53 can identify network bottlenecks and send your traffic along speedier routes.

Virtual Private Cloud

You may want to further segregate your services in AWS for security reasons. Our Cloud9 instance was created in the default **Virtual Private Cloud** (**VPC**). All of the networking components we needed to communicate to those components are in the same VPC. Amazon makes it easy to create multiple clouds. You might provide these to your customers by business unit or have an application per VPC.

Subnets

Subnets provide another mechanism to direct and segregate network traffic. Best practices are to create public and private subnets to prevent unauthorized internet traffic from your secure services. Each subnet will have a gateway. This is the node in your network that knows how to forward packets on to other networks.

Dynamic Host Configuration Protocol

AWS will assign your instances IP addresses by default. An address to help it to resolve DNS will also be provided. These are supplied, along with any other necessary configuration items, by the **Dynamic Host Configuration Protocol** (**DHCP**) service. Amazon permits you to customize these settings too.

Routing

Subnets are denied access to each other by default. You must create a routing table to support communications. Access control lists provide more granular support for locking down permissions.

Peering

VPC peering provides a mechanism for private clouds to speak to each other. These clouds do not have to be owned or managed by the same individuals or companies. AWS also allows peering relationships to be established between (VPCs) across different regions. We'll investigate the benefits of using multiple regions in the next chapter.

Gateways

We talked earlier about how gateways allow networks to talk to each other. AWS also provides some special gateways that simplify building your solutions:

- **Internet gateway**: As the name implies, the **internet gateway (IGW)** provides a single ingress/egress point from your VPC to the public internet.
- **VPN gateway**: A **VPN gateway (VGN)** gives the VPC a single route to a virtual private network. This may be back to your home data center, a partner endpoint, or any connection that requires in-transit encryption.
- **NAT gateway**: The NAT gateway can be used to send all outbound traffic through a single IP address. This reduces the need for public IP addresses for your instances. It lowers the vectors of attack for malicious actors and script-kiddies alike.

Load balancers

In order to achieve web-scale and minimize service interruptions, we recommend you front your services with a **Load Balancer (LB)**. These components take traffic and distribute them across multiple instance or containers. Amazon provides the option to create internal or external (internet facing) load balancers. Internal LBs can decouple DNS or IP address knowledge from service discovery.

Elastic Load Balancer

The **Elastic Load Balancer (ELB)** or Classic LB distributes incoming application or network traffic across multiple targets. Historically, this was done for web servers, but as cloud computing has become more ubiquitous, other services were supported.

The ELB supports all transport layer protocols. It must be used for non-browser-based services.

Application Load Balancer

The **Application Load Balancer (ALB)** is designed specifically for situations where you need to inspect your service traffic. It can redirect requests to different backing instances based upon what it finds during packet inspection. **Hypertext Transport Protocol (HTTP)**, secure HTTP, websockets, and HTTP/2 are excellent candidates for the ALB.

Local traffic manager

In conjunction with DNS, load balancing can be used to ensure you are providing reliable services to your users. We'll plunge into this more in `Chapter 3`, *Availability Patterns - Understanding Your Needs*.

Intrusion detection and prevention services

AWS also can ensure your cloud assets aren't overrun by denial of service attacks. They can also scan for common attack patterns in your inbound traffic.

Shield

The Shield service is enabled for all AWS accounts by default. It protects you against standard **Distributed Denial of Service** (**DDOS**) attacks. There is an advanced version that provides additional configuration options and round-the-clock support.

Web Application Firewall

The **Web Application Firewall** (**WAF**) works in conjunction with Shield. It gives you the ability to create access control lists for your applications. Custom rules can also be configured to audit your traffic. Common rule types, such as those found in the OWASP vulnerabilities list, are built in to the WAF inspection engine.

Storage

Amazon provides a number of highly available, fault tolerant, and durable storage options we can take advantage of in our products. They span the range from block to object storage. Depending on your product needs, you can use them individually, or compose them as needed. Integration with compute, networking, and security services is a common practice. The mature APIs and instrumentation of the services simplify their use.

Elastic Block Storage

Elastic Block Storage (EBS) is the disk type you want to use for the majority of your products. EBS implements a standard block device for EC2 instances. Disks spawned by EBS can be cloned, extended, or attached to other instances. Snapshots can be taken while EBS volumes are in use to ensure **Recovery Time Objectives (RTO)** of data can be met.

Ephemeral

Cloud resources are meant to be short-lived. That is why the default disk for AWS is the ephemeral type. Once the instance it was attached to is deleted, so is the disk. Do not use this type for any data that you want to persist. Persistence practices will be investigated in `Chapter 10`, *Databases – Identifying Which Type Fits Your Needs*, of this book.

Simple Storage Solution

Simple Storage Solution (S3) is the AWS object storage offering. It is not a traditional file system. The different storage classes allow you to store your data close to your compute, or distribute it globally. Life cycle policies can be defined for access control, versioning, encryption, and tagging. Creation and deletion of objects also spawns event streams that can be consumed in your applications.

Glacier

Glacier is the lowest storage class in S3. It is an extremely inexpensive archival solution that takes advantage of Amazon's vast capacity. The read limitations are quite severe as it is intended to be accessed infrequently. Take advantage of Glacier for your audit and compliance storage requirements as it is designed for durability (lack of data loss).

CloudFront

CloudFront is a global **content delivery network (CDN)**. Using S3 as your backend allows you to easily create static webpages with minimal effort and low cost. CloudFront's integrations with other AWS services make it a good starting point for migrating workloads to the cloud.

Elastic File System

Amazon **Elastic File System** (**EFS**) provides a shared filesystem for the cloud. EFS distributed nature helps you to avoid single points of failure across instances. The NFSv4 protocol it supports lets different operating systems mount volumes and treat them as local filesystems.

Amazon Machine Images

Amazon Machine Images (**AMI**) are disk snapshots that you can use or create to avoid toil. Reusing the AWS-provided images gives you a good baseline for building custom solutions. Once those are built, you can create your own AMIs. These can be transferred to other regions and deployed alongside compute to ensure consistency across all of your instances.

IAM

IAM gives you the ability to manage users, their service account, their permissions, and their roles across all your services. In addition, you can create instance-, container-, or function-scoped roles. Federation of existing directory services and single sign-on solutions can also be accomplished using IAM. We'll come back to IAM in `Chapter 4`, *Security - Ensuring the Integrity of Your Systems*.

Security Token Service

The AWS **Security Token Service** (**STS**) is a web service that enables you to request temporary, limited-privilege credentials for IAM users. We'll see why this is a great feature when we cover least privilege security in `Chapter 4`, *Security - Ensuring the Integrity of Your Systems*.

Speaking of least privilege, you really shouldn't be using your root user for AWS console access. Let's create a new user. Then go back and see whether you can recreate your environment with the new user.

Create a file named `user.tf` and add the following:

```
resource "aws_iam_user" "cloudpatterns" {
 name = "loadbalancer"
}

resource "aws_iam_group" "group" {
  name = "cloudpatterngroup"
}

resource "aws_iam_group_membership" "admin" {
 name = "tf-admin-group-membership"
 users = [
   "${aws_iam_user.cloudpatterns.name}",
 ]
 group = "${aws_iam_group.group.name}"
}

resource "aws_iam_group_policy_attachment" "test-attach" {
 group = "${aws_iam_group.group.name}"
 policy_arn = "arn:aws:iam::aws:policy/AdministratorAccess"
}
```

Save it, then run the following:

```
terraform plan
terraform apply -target=aws_iam_user.cloudpatterns
```

You should see your new user in the IAM console.

Summary

In this chapter, we went through some of the AWS components you will use to build your products. We covered source management, compute, storage, networking, and user management. There are many services we did not cover. Some of these, such as databases and machine learning, we will touch on in the remainder of this book. Others, we will omit entirely in order to stay focused on well-used patterns. We will continue to use our instance of Cloud9 throughout this book as our cloud IDE. In the IDE, we installed Terraform and created some AWS resources. Lastly, we focused on how everything we do in AWS can be driven through code and the importance of versioning it.

In the next chapter, we will combine some of the components into architectures aimed towards creating your own highly available services.

Further reading

- *AWS Certified Solutions Architect – Associate Guide* (https://subscription.packtpub.com/book/virtualization_and_cloud/9781789130669) goes into more depth on services not covered in this book.
- The *Hands-On Infrastructure Automation with Terraform on AWS* video (https://subscription.packtpub.com/video/big_data_and_business_intelligence/9781789534849) demonstrates more complex Terraform structures than the ones we will present.
- A comprehensive run-through of the AWS foundational services can be found in the *Learning Amazon Web Services* video (https://subscription.packtpub.com/video/virtualization_and_cloud/9781789341263).
- To learn more about Git for source control, check out the following: https://git-scm.com/.

3
Availability Patterns - Understanding Your Needs

By creating a shared vocabulary, we will establish which patterns can be applied to deliver the necessary availability levels. We will design a stack that can meet your product's service level objectives. Our architecture will be designed to scale and handle failure while minimizing cost and operating close to your customers.

The following topics will be covered in this chapter in brief:

- High availability
- Load balancing
- Fault tolerance
- Auto scaling
- Hierarchical storage management

Technical requirements

The code for this chapter can be found at https://github.com/PacktPublishing/Implementing-Cloud-Design-Patterns-for-AWS-Second-Edition/tree/master/Chapter03.

Please use the Cloud9 console to create a directory called `ch3` and change to it before you begin:

```
mkdir ch3 && cd ch3
```

High availability

One of the primary benefits of the public cloud is its geographical dispersion of resources. This distribution allows you to build highly available solutions at low cost. Availability covers a number of diverse topics. Depending on the customer, it can be measured in different ways. Traditionally, system uptime was the primary indicator. In the pre-cloud era, five nines was a good goal to have. This meant that your systems were up 99.999% of the time; downtime could be no more than five and a half minutes per year. As microservices became more prevalent in the cloud era, and systems got distributed across the globe, five nines became unrealistic. This is because complex systems inherently have more potential failure points and are more difficult to implement correctly. In a simple example with three components, each having five nines, the formula $99.999\%*99.999\%*99.999\% = 99.997\%$ illustrates how traditional measures of uptime start to break down in the cloud.

Amazon S3 has a service level agreement for uptime of 99.9%. This allows for ten minutes of downtime a week. We will call this ten-minute window your error budget. In `Chapter 7`, *Operation and Maintenance – Keeping Things Running at Peak Performance*, we will go into more detail on error budgets plus service level indicators, objectives, and agreements. For this chapter, we will use three nines as our availability goal and measure product availability, not system uptime. Although our examples primarily focus on instances, these same practices should be applied to improve availability of your containerized and functional workloads.

Top-level domain

The first thing most users of your product will encounter is your address or **Uniform Resource Indicator** (**URI**). We will be using the `cloudpatterns.uk` domain for the examples in this book. A URL for this domain would look like `https://my.cloudpatterns.uk`. If you don't have a domain name, now is a good time to create one. There is no API to do this, but you can do it in the UI—this is part of the raison d'être for Route53 (`https://console.aws.amazon.com/route53/home`).

 Obtaining a URI is usually not free. I chose a `.uk` domain for this book because it was the lowest cost option.

Click the **Get started now** button and then the **Register Domain** button on the subsequent page:

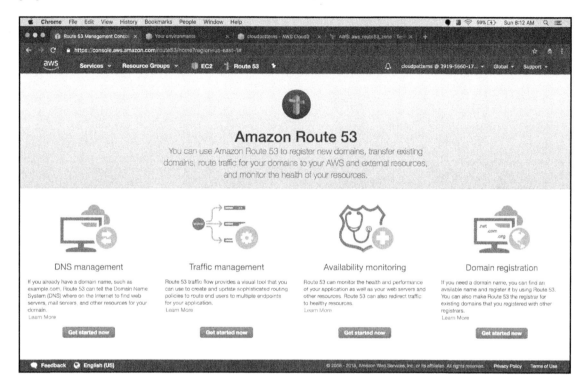

You can also transfer your existing domain to AWS if you already have one:

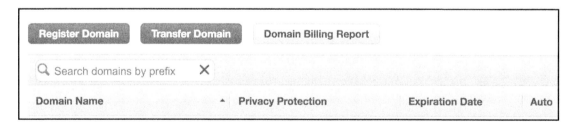

Availability Patterns - Understanding Your Needs

Search for an available domain:

Fill out your contact information and read and agree to the terms of service, then purchase your domain:

It took about ten minutes for me to get my registration confirmation.

 Some registrars may take up to three days.

Amazon will create your root-hosted zone by default. Let's add a subdomain with Terraform. Copy your `main.tf` file to a new folder called `Chapter3` and run `terraform init`:

```
# grab the existing cloudpatterns-zone in Route53
data "aws_route53_zone" "main" {
  name = "cloudpatterns.uk."
}

resource "aws_route53_zone" "book" {
  name = "book.cloudpatterns.uk"

  tags {
    Environment = "book"
  }
}

resource "aws_route53_record" "book-ns" {
```

[48]

```
    zone_id = "${data.aws_route53_zone.main.zone_id}"
    name = "book.cloudpatterns.uk"
    type = "NS"
    ttl = "30"

    records = [
      "${aws_route53_zone.book.name_servers.0}",
      "${aws_route53_zone.book.name_servers.1}",
      "${aws_route53_zone.book.name_servers.2}",
      "${aws_route53_zone.book.name_servers.3}",
    ]
}
```

Create your Terraform plan and apply it. You'll see your new zones in the AWS console:

Domain Name	Type	Record Set Count	Comment	Hosted Zone ID
cloudpatterns.uk.	Public	3	HostedZone created by Route53 Registrar	Z2BO6D0HOPYJGR
book.cloudpatterns.uk.	Public	3	Managed by Terraform	Z3GGUA4HXA5D5A

Click on one to see the records it created:

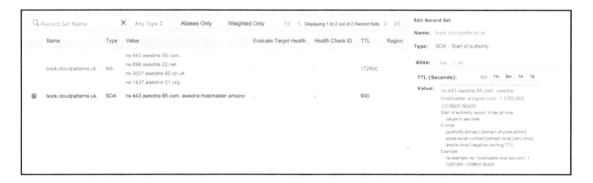

We now are ready to create our globally available product.

Regions

So far, all of our work has been done in the US-East region of AWS. The following map shows that there are a few other options too: `https://aws.amazon.com/about-aws/global-infrastructure/`.

To increase the availability of our product, we'll add another region at the bottom of our `main.tf` file:

```
provider "aws" {
  region = "us-west-2"
  alias = "west"
}
```

A new VPC will allow us to further isolate our resources from tenants within our own organization. Let's create a `vpc.tf` file as follows. We'll keep the network address space the same for simplicity for the moment:

```
resource "aws_vpc" "mainvpc" {
  cidr_block = "10.1.0.0/16"
}

resource "aws_vpc" "mainvpc_west" {
  provider = "aws.west"
  cidr_block = "10.2.0.0/16"
}
```

Now, let's create some new instance resources. We will use the same base AMI in both areas, but put these virtual machines in different regions, also in `vpc.tf`:

```
# Virginia
resource "aws_instance" "cheap_worker" {
  # the below ami is for the latest Bitnami Wordpress East
  ami = "ami-001e1c1159ccfe992"
  instance_type = "t2.micro"
  availability_zone = "us-east-1d"
  associate_public_ip_address = true

  tags {
    Name = "CheapWorker"
  }
}
output "id" {
  value = "${aws_instance.cheap_worker.id}"
}
output "ip" {
  value = "${aws_instance.cheap_worker.public_ip}"
```

```
}

# Oregon
resource "aws_instance" "cheap_worker_west" {
  # the below ami is for the latest Bitnami Wordpress West
  ami = "ami-000ce50ab0df5943f"
  provider = "aws.west"
  instance_type = "t2.micro"
  availability_zone = "us-west-2c"
  associate_public_ip_address = true

  tags {
    Name = "CheapWorker"
  }
}
output "id_west" {
  value = "${aws_instance.cheap_worker_west.id}"
}
output "ip_west" {
  value = "${aws_instance.cheap_worker_west.public_ip}"
}
```

Notice that, even though we are using the same version of WordPress provided by Bitnami, the AMIs are different in the east and west catalogs.

Load balancing

Our instances are running, but there is no way to access them outside of AWS. We will use a classic **Elastic Load Balancing** (**ELB**) for our examples, but the ALB offers a number of additional features for web traffic. These include more advanced health checks, better redirection, and a more complete pool management component.

Global Traffic Manager

In this case, we will use a DNS record to point at the public IP addresses of both instances. This creates a **Global Traffic Manager** (**GTM**) service in front of them by adding this to the bottom of main.tf:

```
# Global Traffic Management using DNS
resource "aws_route53_record" "www" {
  zone_id = "${aws_route53_zone.book.zone_id}"
```

Availability Patterns - Understanding Your Needs

```
    name = "www.book.cloudpatterns.cuk"
    type = "A"
    ttl = "300"
    records = [
      "${aws_instance.cheap_worker.public_ip}",
      "${aws_instance.cheap_worker_west.public_ip}"
    ]
}
```

Run your `terraform plan` command and then `terraform apply -auto-approve` (since I'm getting tired of typing `yes` at the prompt). You should see an instance running in each region and a new DNS record in Route 53. Let's try to access the `https://www.book.cloudpatterns.uk` URL. The Bitnami image listens on port `80` and `443` by default, but you can't get to them! We need to allow inbound traffic on the HTTP(S) ports. Let's create our first security groups. We want one in each region—use `vpc.tf` for this:

```
resource "aws_default_security_group" "default" {
  vpc_id = "${aws_vpc.mainvpc.id}"
  ingress {
    from_port = 80
    to_port = 80
    protocol = "tcp"
    cidr_blocks = ["0.0.0.0/0"]
  }
```

```
  egress {
    from_port = 0
    to_port = 0
    protocol = "-1"
    cidr_blocks = ["0.0.0.0/0"]
  }
}

resource "aws_default_security_group" "default_west" {
  vpc_id = "${aws_vpc.mainvpc_west.id}"
  provider = "aws.west"
  ingress {
    from_port = 80
    to_port = 80
    protocol = "tcp"
    cidr_blocks = ["0.0.0.0/0"]
  }
```

```
  egress {
```

```
        from_port = 0
        to_port = 0
        protocol = "-1"
        cidr_blocks = ["0.0.0.0/0"]
    }
}
```

Chapter 4, *Security - Ensuring the Integrity of Your Systems*, will explain what's happening in that code. Re-run your plan and apply it. Refresh your browser and you should see the welcome screen:

Now you have a globally distributed WordPress deployment. Unfortunately, you have to wait until the *Persistence Patterns* section for us to be able to keep the data synchronized.

To deliver content to end users with lower latency, Amazon CloudFront uses a global network of 136 Points of Presence (125 Edge Locations and 11 Regional Edge Caches) in 62 cities across 29 countries (correct at time of writing). Lambda Edge Functions also take advantage of these local POPs.

Availability Zones

You'll notice that, in the instance creation code, I specified an **Availability Zone** *(AZ)* where the instance should reside. AZs in AWS map to local failure domains. Most regions have multiple AZs, as you can see from the previous map. The following diagram shows how AZs are connected by low-latency links within a region: `https://docs.aws.amazon.com/AWSEC2/latest/UserGuide/using-regions-availability-zones.html`.

We jumped ahead a little bit to get global availability of our product. Local availability should have been the first step. It provides some additional benefits that simplify our architecture. We're going to build another Terraform instance resource and deploy it into `AZ 1C` in the **us-east1** region. Let's create a new Terraform file and call it `instanceAZ1c.tf`:

```
# Virginia 1c
resource "aws_instance" "cheap_worker1c" {
  # the below ami is for the latest Bitnami Wordpress East
  ami = "ami-001e1c1159ccfe992"
  instance_type = "t2.micro"
  availability_zone = "us-east-1c"

  tags {
    Name = "CheapWorker"
  }
}
output "id1c" {
  value = "${aws_instance.cheap_worker1c.id}"
}
```

Run your plan and apply. Notice that we didn't create a public IP for this instance. This reduces my attack surface and is generally the best practice. We'll see how to make this instance public facing in the *Local Traffic Management* section next.

Local Traffic Management

Our regional AWS load balancers can provide **Local Traffic Management** (**LTM**) services. By adding a layer of abstraction between DNS and our instances, we can take advantage of a number of patterns for maintaining our backing services with little or no downtime.

Chapter 6, *Ephemeral Environments - Sandboxes for Experiments*, will go into detail about those architectures, but for now, we will add our latest instance to the load balancer, then update DNS (our GTM) to point to our load balancer (our LTM) in addition to the existing instances—see the following changes made to the `instanceAZ1c.tf` file:

```
# Create a new load balancer
resource "aws_elb" "cloudelb" {
  name = "cloudpatterns-elb"
  availability_zones = ["us-east-1c"]

  listener {
    instance_port = 80
    instance_protocol = "http"
    lb_port = 80
    lb_protocol = "http"
  }

  health_check {
    healthy_threshold = 2
    unhealthy_threshold = 2
    timeout = 3
    target = "HTTP:80/"
    interval = 30
  }

  instances = ["${aws_instance.cheap_worker1c.id}"]
  cross_zone_load_balancing = true
  idle_timeout = 400
  connection_draining = true
  connection_draining_timeout = 400
}
```

Remove the `aws_route53_record.www` resource configuration from the `main.tf` file. Then, we'll destroy the A record used in the environment by performing the following instruction in the `terraform destroy target=aws_route53_record.www` bash panel. Now we will need to add a different type of DNS record; we'll create a new file called `ltm.tf`:

```
# Global Traffic Management using DNS
resource "aws_route53_record" "wwwltm" {
  zone_id = "${aws_route53_zone.book.zone_id}"
  name = "www"
  type = "cname"
  ttl = "300"
  records = ["${aws_elb.cloudelb.dns_name}"]
}
```

[55]

Plan and apply your Terraform to get your new CNAME record:

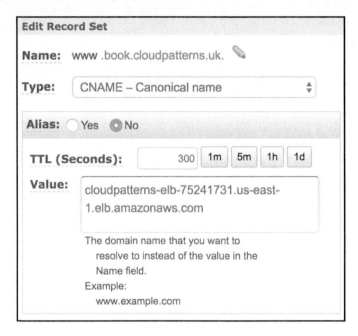

You will notice that your WordPress is still responding. The canonical name record allows us to point one DNS record at another. Using this pointer, AWS can scale our load balancer (LTM) up and down without us worrying about the ever-changing IP addresses. We can do the same thing with our service instances.

 Now would be a good time to commit your code and push it with Git.

Health checks

The other great item the AWS load balancers provide is a health checking feature. In our previous small-scale example, there is only one instance. The load balancer checks every thirty seconds for a valid response from the HTTP port. If three checks fail, it removes the instance from the pool. This helps to insulate us from any individual faults in our services. This works a lot better when we have multiple instances attached to our load balancer.

Fault tolerance

Power outages, hardware failures, and data center upgrades are just a few of the many problems that still bubble up to the engineering teams responsible for systems. Data center upgrades are common, and given enough time at AWS, your product team will get an email or notification stating that some servers will shut down, or experience brownouts, or small outages of power. We've shown that the best way to handle these is to span across data centers (AZs) so that, if a single location experiences issues, the systems will continue to respond. Your services should be configured in an *N+1* configuration. If a single frontend is acceptable, then it should be configured for two. Spanning AZs gives us further protection from large-scale outages while keeping latency low. This allows for hiccups and brownouts, as well as an influx of traffic into the system with minimal impact to the end users.

An example of this architecture can be seen in the reference architecture for Cloud Foundry (http://www.cloudfoundry.org). Each subnet is in a different AZ. Components are deployed on each subnet to provide fault tolerance. A complete loss of two Amazon data centers would slow the system down, but it would continue to be available: https://docs.pivotal.io/pivotalcf/2-1/plan/aws/aws_ref_arch.html.

We can see how DNS is used for global traffic management and a set of load balancers creates a facade for LTM.

Auto scaling

If you've applied the patterns and followed the practices enumerated here, you are on the road to success. Unfortunately, success often comes more swiftly than you expect. A mention on Hacker News, Reddit, or Twitter can send waves of traffic your way. Let's take a look at how Amazon's auto scaling feature can help us to meet the demand in a cost effective way. First, we will define a launch configuration for our product—this should go into the `instanceAZ1c.tf` file:

```
resource "aws_launch_configuration" "asg_conf" {
  name = "book-asg-config"
  image_id = "ami-001e1c1159ccfe992"
  instance_type = "t2.micro"
}
```

Then, add an autoscaling group to the same file, which encompasses all AZs, so that the workload gets distributed evenly:

```
resource "aws_autoscaling_group" "book_group" {
  availability_zones = ["us-east-1a","us-east-1b","us-east-1c"]
  name = "book-group-asg"
  max_size = 5
  min_size = 2
  health_check_grace_period = 300
  health_check_type = "ELB"
  force_delete = true
  launch_configuration = "${aws_launch_configuration.asg_conf.name}"
}
```

And add a policy that defines the configuration for capacity, causes, adjustment, and cool down, which in this case puts the policy to sleep for an arbitrary five minutes:

```
resource "aws_autoscaling_policy" "bat" {
  name = "book-policy-ASG"
  scaling_adjustment = 4
  adjustment_type = "ChangeInCapacity"
  cooldown = 300
  autoscaling_group_name = "${aws_autoscaling_group.book_group.name}"
}
```

Placement groups

To further distribute your load across physical hardware, you can create a placement group. The following resource will cause your instance to be spread across underlying hardware:

```
resource "aws_placement_group" "web" {
  name = "book-pg"
  strategy = "spread"
}
```

Add the following to your instance resources to spread them across underlying hardware:

```
placement_group = "book-pg"
```

> You could also use the cluster strategy to a create a low-latency instance group in a single AZ.

Hierarchical storage management

S3 can be configured to use global or local buckets. Investigate your latency requirements before choosing the global option. You can use replication to synchronize your objects across regions if eventual consistency is acceptable—the following code sample shows how this might be achieved, but should not be used verbatim:

```
{
  "Version": "2012-10-17",
  "Statement": [
    {
      "Action": [
        "s3:GetReplicationConfiguration",
        "s3:ListBucket"
      ],
      "Effect": "Allow",
      "Resource": [
        "${aws_s3_bucket.bucket.arn}"
      ]
    },
```

```
resource "aws_iam_policy_attachment" "replication" {
  name = "tf-iam-role-attachment-replication-12345"
  roles = ["${aws_iam_role.replication.name}"]
  policy_arn = "${aws_iam_policy.replication.arn}"
}

resource "aws_s3_bucket" "destination" {
  bucket = "tf-test-bucket-destination-12345"
  region = "us-west-1"

  versioning {
    enabled = true
  }
}
```

```
  replication_configuration {
    role = "${aws_iam_role.replication.arn}"

    rules {
      id = "foobar"
      prefix = "foo"
      status = "Enabled"

      destination {
```

```
            bucket        = "${aws_s3_bucket.destination.arn}"
            storage_class = "STANDARD"
          }
        }
      }
    }
```

The complete version of the preceding code block can be found in the GitHub page: https://github.com/PacktPublishing/Implementing-Cloud-Design-Patterns-for-AWS-Second-Edition/tree/master/Chapter03.

Storage life cycle policies can also be attached to your buckets, which will move infrequently accessed object to less available and more inexpensive storage:

```
resource "aws_s3_bucket" "versioning_bucket" {
  bucket = "my-versioning-bucket"
  acl = "private"

  versioning {
    enabled = true
  }

  lifecycle_rule {
    prefix = "config/"
    enabled = true
    noncurrent_version_transition {
      days = 30
      storage_class = "STANDARD_IA"
    }

    noncurrent_version_transition {
      days = 60
      storage_class = "GLACIER"
    }

    noncurrent_version_expiration {
      days = 90
    }
  }
}
```

Remember that, even though read speeds and bandwidth decrease with lower storage classes, object durability remains very high (such as ten nines).

Summary

In this chapter, we discussed patterns to help to reduce downtime due to faults and increase availability. We also discussed a few patterns that help to create more resilient tiers that can withstand AZ and regional outages. Finally, we looked at how you can use S3 policies to afford your storage these same benefits. We strongly recommend injecting failures into your production systems regularly and will broach the topic again in Chapter 6, *Ephemeral Environments – Sandboxes for Experiments*.

In the upcoming chapter, we will discuss patterns to keep your systems well defended in order to further boost uptime.

 Use `terraform destroy` any time you don't want to leave your resources running up the bill.

Exercises

1. Add some additional instances to your ELB.
2. Create a second load balancer in the west.
3. Update your DNS record to include the new load balancer.
4. Add some instances in different AZs in the west.
5. Change your security group to allow only ingress from your IP address.
6. Apply the security group to your ELBs instead of your instances.

Further reading

- *Reliability and Resilience on AWS* (https://subscription.packtpub.com/video/virtualization_and_cloud/9781789611700) digs deeper into the load balancing options offered by Amazon.
- The fifth chapter of *Cloud Native Architectures* (https://subscription.packtpub.com/book/application_development/9781787280540) presents more generalized patterns for availability in the cloud.
- *Managing Mission-Critical Domains and DNS* (https://subscription.packtpub.com/book/networking_and_servers/9781789135077) delves broadly into the importance of domains.

4
Security - Ensuring the Integrity of Your Systems

In this chapter, we will address a concern that touches on all aspects of your product. Security best practices will be covered. The three tenets of security are confidentiality, integrity, and availability. Methods we will touch upon that will help you in lowering operational risk, increasing transport layer security, simplifying user and role management, and implementing least privileges while establishing an audit trail for your product. Confidentiality addresses how we protect our data, in motion and at rest, from unauthorized access. This will allow us to establish a perimeter around all of our products from the start. Integrity focuses on the accuracy of our data. We will address different data types in the *Persistence Patterns* section, and so we will generalize in this chapter.

In this chapter, we will cover the following topics:

- Key management service
- Credentials
- RBAC
- Cognito
- Enterprise integrations
- Logging
- Vulnerability scanning

Technical requirements

The code for this chapter can be found at `https://github.com/PacktPublishing/Implementing-Cloud-Design-Patterns-for-AWS-Second-Edition/ch4`.

Please use the Cloud9 console to create a directory called `ch4` and change to it before you begin:

```
mkdir ch4 && cd ch4
```

Shared responsibilities

A huge benefit of using AWS services is that they manage a great deal of the security for you. You get to focus on product concerns. Amazon's data centers have certification for compliance with a large number of global standards such as CSA and ISO 27001. They also have industry-specific certifications for PCI, HIPAA, and NIST. Customers who trust AWS to house their products range from the Fortune 1000 to local governments.

Cloud specific

Building your product on the cloud lets you concentrate on the features that are important to your customer. We have been using AWS APIs (wrapped by Terraform) to manage our deployments. Amazon manages the security of, and access to, all physical devices. Assessments and testing of their assets are part of their ongoing operational concerns. Vulnerability and patch management for any hardware bugs (such as Spectre and Meltdown) are covered by their service-level agreements. However, operating systems and some services will require upgrades on your part. The same pattern applies to communication and network security. Physical devices and their interconnections are protected by Amazon. We have been using the AWS APIs (wrapped by Terraform) to manage our deployments. Those are secured by **Transport Layer Security** (**TLS**) using an Amazon certificate. All of the components added into your VPC must be managed by you.

Governance

Governance consists of accountability, defining decision rights, and balancing benefits or values, risk, and resources in an environment. Cloud governance practices should be no different than your current methods. Your product architecture should be designed to minimize risk, limit access privileges, and provide a way to trace user and system actions.

Risk

It is impossible to mitigate all potential risks. If you eliminate public access to your product, you will see a major decline in your revenue. So you must balance risk levels with potential impact on your business. Data security regulations, on-demand self-service, broad network access, resource pooling, rapid elasticity, and measured services are some of the concerns that affect availability, integrity, and confidentiality. A multi-tenant design lets AWS provide you with very low-cost resources. Using shared compute may make sense in development environments where mock customer data exists, whereas dedicated instances can limit exposure when real-world data is present. More detailed approaches will be covered throughout this chapter.

Add this snippet to your instance resource if you want dedicated instances:

```
...
tenancy: dedicated
...
```

Compliance

We touched on some of the certifications AWS holds earlier. Your product may need further controls in place to gain certification. Data segregation, a key component of the EU's **General Data Protection Regulation** (**GDPR**) can be achieved by keeping your product in a single territory. The **Infrastructure as Code** (**IaC**) strategy makes it easy to scale globally while keeping resources consistent and regional. Other high-level methods discussed next will illustrate how to reuse compliant practices across your product line.

More information on specific programs can be found on the AWS compliance site at https://aws.amazon.com/compliance/.

Inheritance

Beyond the derived controls you get by using AWS, one of the best ways to enforce good security practices is to reuse your AWS policies. By creating user and instance roles, you are able to assign specific policies at creation time. Later in the chapter, we will talk more about how to ensure that non-standard policies and roles can be prevented through real-time inspection of objects during instantiation. Also, in the *Credentials* section, we will look at audit practices that will help us to identify any gaps in our roles and policies.

Defense in depth

So far, we have addressed security procedures that can be configured before your product exists. We are going to shift gears to more practical matters now. A layered defense of your product provides the best buffer against breaches of confidential data, malicious denial-of-service attacks against your availability, and the alteration of your systems for pernicious purposes. A combination of physical, virtual, and procedural controls will limit your risk throughout the **Software Development Life Cycle (SDLC)**.

Least privilege

Do not give everyone administrator access to your systems. If possible, don't give anyone access at all. Roles and policies should be applied at the finest grained level possible. A user who needs to see how many object exist in an S3 bucket does not need read or write permissions. Developers generally need full access to non-production environments, but rarely need the same level in production settings.

Users

As with every other piece of our product management effort, users, the roles they have, and the groups they belong to can be defined in code. Roles, also software defined, should be attached to groups. By using groups, we simplify the maintenance process down the road. The elimination of unnecessary activities (toil) will be assessed in `Chapter 7`, *Operation and Maintenance - Keeping Things Running at Peak Performance*. A common practice is to have non-real users or service accounts to manage interprocess communications. These accounts should follow all of the same practices outlined earlier. Identifying your product personas can help you to map access privileges to the right people. Typical personas you will have to address include the software engineer, reliability engineer, and customer. By generalizing these personas into IAM groups, your security can be consistent across all users. Always remember that AWS is API-driven; minimize access to endpoints whenever possible through roles.

In transit

The APIs are secured through TLS. Any products you are publicly exposing should take advantage of TLS security too. We will cover how to obtain certificates from Amazon for use on your internet-facing load balancers in a bit. We do recommend that all of the microservices that make up your product use transit encryption.

Many of the AWS services allow configuration of encryption at creation. We will select the encryption features in all of the AWS services we use throughout this book. Generally, we try to avoid the ones that don't allow enabling the services. If an attacker does manage to gain control of, or create, an instance in your environment, sniffing your encrypted traffic will give them no further information.

VPC

The goal is to not let anyone get into your cloud. The VPC provides us with more opportunities to reduce our attack vectors. A combination of private addresses, traffic segregation, and filtering plus **Access Control Lists** (**ACL**) adds to our product fortification. The ability to use AWS internal service endpoints, or create custom VPC ones, stops our packets from traversing any public networks.

Security groups – port filtering

In the same way we created user groups in IAM, we can create **Security Groups** (**SG**) in our VPC. The primary focus of our SGs is to provide a mechanism to enforce port filtering. This is a very granular level of enforcement within the private cloud:

```
# Add a security group to our load balancer
resource "aws_elb" "cloudelb" {
  name = "cloudpatterns-elb"
  availability_zones = ["us-east-1c"]
  security_groups = ["default"]

  listener {
    ...
  connection_draining_timeout = 400

}
```

We will be using ellipses to indicate that code has been removed for the remainder of this book. Added code will be in bold.

A secondary benefit of the SG is that it allows for inter-SG communications. In the same manner as user groups, adding an instance, container, or function into an SG allows the object to inherit all of the rights of the group. Changes to the SG are also applied to all objects simultaneously.

Security - Ensuring the Integrity of Your Systems

Network ACLs – subnet

A higher-grained implementation of security is the network ACL. These ACLs are applied at the subnet level. In conjunction with traditional routing tables, we are adding another preventative measure within our VPC. We could, for example, implement it in the following manner:

```
resource "aws_network_acl" "main" {
  vpc_id = "${aws_vpc.main.id}"

  egress {
    protocol = "tcp"
    rule_no = 200
    action = "allow"
    cidr_block = "10.3.0.0/18"
    from_port = 443
    to_port = 443
  }

  ingress {
    protocol = "tcp"
    rule_no = 100
    action = "allow"
    cidr_block = "10.3.0.0/18"
    from_port = 80
    to_port = 80
  }

  tags {
    Name = "main"
  }
}
```

The following example will pull the subnet IDs from our VPC, create two gateways for egress, and allow our first subnet to use it. The second gateway will allow outbound IPv6 traffic from any network in our VPC:

```
data "aws_subnet_ids" "default_subnet_ids" {
  vpc_id = "${aws_vpc.mainvpc.id}"
}

resource "aws_egress_only_internet_gateway" "ipv6_gw" {
  vpc_id = "${aws_vpc.mainvpc.id}"
}

resource "aws_nat_gateway" "nat_gw" {
  allocation_id = "${aws_eip.nat.id}"
  subnet_id = "${aws_subnet.default_subnets_ids[0]}"
```

```
}
resource "aws_route_table" "r" {
  vpc_id = "${aws_vpc.default.id}"

  route {
    cidr_block = "0.0.0.0/0"
    gateway_id = "${aws_nat_gateway.nat_gw.id}"
  }

  route {
    ipv6_cidr_block = "::/0"
    egress_only_gateway_id =
"${aws_egress_only_internet_gateway.ipv6_gw.id}"
  }
}
```

Obscurity

A collateral benefit of using a **Network Address Translation** (**NAT**) gateway is that all of our outbound traffic will appear to come from a single IP. By cloaking our actual address from the public view, we further complicate intruder efforts.

> All of your outbound traffic should also be using TLS encryption (or a suitable equivalent).

Come to think of it, we have done the same thing with all of our inbound traffic. While our ELB isn't primarily meant to hide our addresses, it needs to use NAT to balance traffic to internal services. Our final method to avoid getting fingerprinted by hackers is to use internal endpoints for S3 and EC2. That way, we will not be sending any service calls to public networks:

```
resource "aws_vpc_endpoint" "s3" {
  vpc_id = "${aws_vpc.main.id}"
  service_name = "com.amazonaws.us-east-1.s3"
}
```

Application

Now we finally get to secure our WordPress instance with public-facing TLS encryption. We will add a certificate from the **Amazon Certificate Manager** (**ACM**) and attach it to our load balancer on port 443:

```
# Create a wildcard certificate using Amazon Certificate Manager
resource "aws_acm_certificate" "cloudpatterns_cert" {
  domain_name = "www.book.cloudpatterns.co.uk"
  validation_method = "DNS"

  tags {
    Environment = "test"
  }

  lifecycle {
    create_before_destroy = true
  }
}
...
listener {
  instance_port = 80
  instance_protocol = "http"
  lb_port = 443
  lb_protocol = "https"
  ssl_certificate_id = "${aws_acm_certificate.cloudpatterns_cert.id}"
}
```

To further improve our security, we should add the AWS **web application firewall** (**WAF**) to our ELB. This will also activate the Shield service to protect us from **Distributed Denial of Service** (**DDoS**) attacks. Unfortunately, the AWS Terraform provider doesn't support mapping WAF regional rules to ELBs. We will have to swap out our ELB for an ALB (better anyway). So, firstly, we're going to set up the ALB by adding in a new resource, setting up a listener, and attaching it to a target group:

```
#create an alb
resource "aws_lb" "book_alb" {
  name = "book_alb"
  subnets = ["${aws_subnet.default_subnets_ids[0]}"]
}

# we need a listener
resource "aws_lb_listener" "front_end" {
  load_balancer_arn = "${aws_lb.book_alb.arn}"
  port = 443
  protocol = "HTTPS"
```

```
    ssl_policy = "ELBSecurityPolicy-2015-05"
    certificate_arn = "${aws_acm_certificate.cloudpatterns_cert.id}"
    default_action {
      type = "forward"
      target_group_arn = "${aws_lb_target_group.book_front_end.arn}"
    }
  }

  resource "aws_lb_target_group" "book_targetgroup" {
    name = "book-lb-tg"
    port = 80
    protocol = "HTTP"
    vpc_id = "${aws_vpc.main.id}"
  }

  resource "aws_lb_target_group_attachment" "lb_target_attach" {
    target_group_arn = "${aws_lb_target_group.book_targetgroup.arn}"
    target_id = "${aws_instance.cheap_worker1c.id}"
    port = 80
  }
```

Now, we're going to set up the WAF—in this case, we're setting up a blacklist to block access to the localhost (or loopback) address. We create a predicate that is passed into a ruleset, which gets blocked when the predicate is true, and finally associates it with the previously created ALB:

```
  # we're going to block the loopback address for this example
  resource "aws_wafregional_ipset" "loopbackipset" {
    name = "tfIPSet"
    ip_set_descriptor {
      type = "IPV4"
      value = "127.0.0.1/8"
    }
  }

  resource "aws_wafregional_rule" "book_wafrule" {
    name = "book_WAFRule"
    metric_name = "book_WAFRule"
    predicate {
      data_id = "${aws_wafregional_ipset.loopbackipset.id}"
      negated = false
      type = "IPMatch"
    }
  }

  resource "aws_wafregional_web_acl" "book_wafacl" {
    name = "bookwafacl"
    metric_name = "bookwafacl"
```

```
    default_action {
      type = "ALLOW"
    }
    rule {
      action {
        type = "BLOCK"
      }
      priority = 1
      rule_id = "${aws_wafregional_rule.bookwafrule.id}"
    }
}

resource "aws_wafregional_web_acl_association" "book_wafacl_association" {
  resource_arn = "${aws_alb.book_alb.arn}"
  web_acl_id = "${aws_wafregional_web_acl.bookwafacl.id}"
}
```

Now we've got an HTTPS load balancer with a valid certificate in front of our WordPress instance. Defense in depth is in place to forestall unauthorized access and outbound NATing to conceal our true addresses. Don't forget to destroy your ELB after you replan and apply.

Terraform is open source. Be a part of the OSS community; go out there and contribute an association resource for the ELB.

At rest

At present, none of our data is classified so that it needs to be cloaked. However, we do have some simple options available for increasing our data privacy. Our instances are using an ephemeral disk, so all of our data will disappear when the instance is removed. When we use persistent storage and databases in the third part of this book, we will encrypt their data as well. Any S3 objects will be secured in the same manner. As we begin to create our own application artifacts, container images, and functions, we will create a checksum to help us to detect integrity errors which may have been introduced during their transmission or storage. In Chapter 12, *Observability - Understanding How Your Products are Behaving*, we will dip into creating and analyzing audit trails to identify any other potential cases of tampering.

Credentials

AWS Secrets Manager enables you to audit and monitor secrets via integration with AWS logging, monitoring, and notification services. For example, after enabling AWS CloudTrail for an AWS region, you can audit when a secret is stored or rotated by viewing AWS CloudTrail logs. Similarly, you can configure Amazon CloudWatch to receive email messages using the Amazon Simple Notification Service when secrets remain unused for a period, or you can configure Amazon CloudWatch Events to receive push notifications when Secrets Manager rotates your secrets:

```
resource "aws_secretsmanager_secret" "rotation-example" {
  name = "rotation-example"
  rotation_lambda_arn = "${aws_lambda_function.example.arn}"

  rotation_rules {
    automatically_after_days = 7
  }
}
```

Here is a key value example:

```
# The map here can come from other supported configurations
# like locals, resource attribute, map() built-in, etc.
variable "example" {
  default = {
    key1 = "value1"
    key2 = "value2"
  }

  type = "map"
}

resource "aws_secretsmanager_secret_version" "example" {
  secret_id = "${aws_secretsmanager_secret.example.id}"
  secret_string = "${jsonencode(var.example)}"
}
```

> Regardless of whether you use AWS Secrets Manager or not, you need a secure location for your credentials. Git is not the answer. Please do not put private information into source code. We have seen many instances where an inadvertent push to a public repository has exposed AWS secrets.

One of the advantages of using a secrets management service is the ability to easily rotate your values on a regular basis. If you don't think it is important to change your passwords regularly, a secrets manager will accelerate the process of creating alternate ones when yours are compromised. In part three, we will integrate Secrets Manager with Amazon RDS.

Certificates

These same practices need to be applied to your certificates as well. Remembering to switch certificates is more important than password rotation because of a built-in expiration date. In the preceding code for our HTTPS load balancer, the life cycle block allowed you to easily swap a new certificate. The Amazon Certificate Manager will remove the old certificate after the new one is provisioned and is in place on the correct resource. You can also import your own certificates as needed:

```
resource "aws_iam_server_certificate" "book_cert_alt" {
  name = "book_test_cert"

  certificate_body = <<EOF
-----BEGIN CERTIFICATE-----
[......] # cert contents
-----END CERTIFICATE-----
EOF

  private_key = <<EOF
-----BEGIN RSA PRIVATE KEY-----
[......] # cert contents
-----END RSA PRIVATE KEY-----
EOF
}
```

Keys

The secrets and certificate services can also coordinate with the AWS **Key Management Service** (**KMS**). The rotation, auditing, and durability features are very similar to the previous services. Enabling automatic key rotation provides the following benefits:

- The properties of the CMK, including its key ID, key ARN, region, policies, and permissions, do not change when the key is rotated.
- You do not need to change applications or aliases that refer to the CMK ID or ARN.

- After you enable key rotation, AWS KMS rotates the CMK automatically every year. You don't need to remember or schedule the update:

```
resource "aws_kms_key" "book_key" {
  description = "KMS key 1"
  deletion_window_in_days = 10
  enable_key_rotation = true
}
```

KMS keys can be used to create certificates for secure communications, encrypt your data at rest (S3, EBS, RDS, EFS, CloudTrail), and protect your source code and its delivery to your cloud:

```
#Create a book bucket
resource "aws_s3_bucket" "mybookbucket" {
  bucket = "mybucket"
  server_side_encryption_configuration {
    rule {
      apply_server_side_encryption_by_default {
        kms_master_key_id = "${aws_kms_key.book_key.arn}"
        sse_algorithm = "aws:kms"
      }
    }
  }
}
```

We will explore more bucket options in the next chapter.

CloudHSM

If your product must adhere with very strict compliance standards, you should consider a hardware security module. AWS' CloudHSM enables you to programmatically manage your keys and export them if necessary. As with their other hardware offerings, AWS monitors the health and network availability of your HSMs, patches software, ensures high availability, and backs up your data. Amazon is not able to create or maintain keys on the CloudHSM device.

RBAC

Circling back to **role-based access control** (**RBAC**) now, we have touched on the importance of user, group, and role management in previous parts of this book, so let's look at how we can implement these elements in Terraform.

Directory service

If you are familiar with Microsoft Active Directory or have existing group policies you would like to apply, the AWS Directory Service will let you easily migrate your objects to the cloud. In most cases, we won't actually move them, but federate our cloud directory services with an existing directory, giving current users and groups access to the AWS Management Console and APIs:

```
resource "aws_directory_service_directory" "bar" {
  name = "corp.notexample.com"
  password = "SuperSecretPassw0rd"
  edition = "Standard"
  type = "MicrosoftAD"

  vpc_settings {
    vpc_id = "${aws_vpc.main.id}"
    subnet_ids = ["${aws_subnet.foo.id}", "${aws_subnet.bar.id}"]
  }
}
```

You should enable secure directory access on your service (LDAPS). As this is important I recommend reading the blog post at `https://aws.amazon.com/blogs/security/how-to-enable-ldaps-for-your-aws-microsoft-ad-directory/`. We're not going to be using Directory Services because our product is not going to need it. But we will be obtaining many of its services through our IAM and Cognito implementations.

More IAM

Before going any further, to gain an extra layer of protection for your cloud, we recommend you enable multi-factor authentication for all of your users. In addition to something they know, users are required to provide something they have (a token). In combination with a fingerprint scanner on a smartphone (something they have), MFA lessens the probability of compromised credentials.

Terraform is unable to set up MFA, but you can do it in the console or with the AWS CLI using the following command:

```
aws iam enable-mfa-device
--user-name <value>
--serial-number <value>
--authentication-code1 <value>
--authentication-code2 <value>
[--cli-input-json <value>]
[--generate-cli-skeleton <value>]
```

We are not going to automate this as the values must be obtained from a physical device in most cases.

> The supported device list can be found here: https://aws.amazon.com/iam/details/mfa/.

Users

We covered Active Directory integration, but what about other options? For our product, cloud engineers are not going to be a large group. We can use the AWS native functionality. However, we will touch on **Single Sign On (SSO)** later in this chapter:

```
resource "aws_iam_user_group_membership" "example1" {
  user = "${aws_iam_user.user1.name}"

  groups = [
    "${aws_iam_group.group1.name}",
    "${aws_iam_group.group2.name}",
  ]
}
```

IAM access policies can be scoped to a single resource, such as the API, a bucket, or all instances. Policies should be attached to a group for inheritance by users (including service-accounts):

```
resource "aws_iam_group_policy" "my_developer_policy" {
  name = "my_developer_policy"
  group = "${aws_iam_group.my_developers.id}"

  policy = <<EOF
{
  "Version": "2012-10-17",
```

```
    "Statement": [
      {
        "Action": [
          "ec2:Describe*"
        ],
        "Effect": "Allow",
        "Resource": "*"
      }
    ]
}
EOF
}

resource "aws_iam_role_policy_attachment" "test-attach" {
  role = "${aws_iam_role.role.name}"
  policy_arn = "${aws_iam_policy.policy.arn}"
}
```

Instance profiles

Policies should be attached to a role for inheritance by instances:

```
resource "aws_iam_role" "book_role" {
  name = "book_role"

  assume_role_policy = <<EOF
{
  "Version": "2012-10-17",
  "Statement": [
    {
      "Effect": "Allow",
      "Action": [ "iam:PassRole", "iam:ListInstanceProfiles", "ec2:*" ],
      "Resource": "*"
    }
  ]
}
EOF
}

resource "aws_iam_instance_profile" "book_instance_profile" {
  name = "book_instance_profile"
  role = "${aws_iam_role.book_role.name}"
}
```

In the preceding example, we specified the `iam:PassRole`. This ensures that a user does not gain elevated privileges when logged on to an instance that has more rights than them. A better solution is for the instance to create a token with just enough authority for the specific operation to happen.

Cognito

If you would like to define and manage credentials for your product users instead of your cloud, Amazon Cognito offers up the ability to define roles and map users to them. This means that your app can access only the resources that are authorized for each user. Cognito supports MFA and encryption of data at rest and in-transit. Integrations with OAuth 2.0, SAML 2.0, and OpenID Connect provide federation options with social media and enterprise SSO providers.

User pools

In order to implement role management with Cognito, we first need to create a pool for our users, as in the following example:

```
resource "aws_cognito_user_pool" "pool" {
  name = "pool"
}

resource "aws_cognito_user_pool_client" "client" {
  name = "client"
  user_pool_id = "${aws_cognito_user_pool.pool.id}"
}
```

Identity pools

Then, we need to map any external identity providers that we wish to use:

```
resource "aws_iam_saml_provider" "default" {
  name = "my-saml-provider"
  saml_metadata_document = "${file("saml-metadata.xml")}"
}

resource "aws_cognito_identity_pool" "main" {
  identity_pool_name = "identity pool"
  allow_unauthenticated_identities = false
```

```
  cognito_identity_providers {
    client_id = "6lhlkkfbfb4q5kpp90urffae"
    provider_name = "cognito-idp.us-east-1.amazonaws.com/us-east-1_Tv0493apJ"
    server_side_token_check = false
  }

  supported_login_providers {
    "graph.facebook.com" = "7346241598935552"
    "accounts.google.com" = "123456789012.apps.googleusercontent.com"
  }

  saml_provider_arns = ["${aws_iam_saml_provider.default.arn}"]
  openid_connect_provider_arns = ["arn:aws:iam::123456789012:oidc-provider/foo.example.com"]
}
```

Full version of the preceding code block is available at: https://github.com/PacktPublishing/Implementing-Cloud-Design-Patterns-for-AWS-Second-Edition

Logging

Logging provides us with insight into the availability and integrity of our clouds.

CloudTrail

CloudTrail captures and records account activity:

```
resource "aws_cloudtrail" "example" {
  name = "tf-trail-foobar"
  s3_bucket_name = "${aws_s3_bucket.mybookbucket.id}"
  s3_key_prefix = "prefix"
  include_global_service_events = false
  kms_key_id : "${aws_kms_key.book_key.id}"

  event_selector {
    read_write_type = "All"
    include_management_events = true

    data_resource {
      type = "AWS::S3::Object"
      values = ["arn:aws:s3:::"]
```

            }
        }
    }

CloudWatch events

CloudWatch is primarily used for monitoring your cloud. It should be used to capture metrics and has nice dashboarding features available in the console. Streaming the events to logs is a good idea. Events can also be based on flow logs and CloudTrail logs:

```
resource "aws_cloudwatch_log_group" "book_log_group" {
  name = "book_log_group"
}

resource "aws_cloudwatch_log_stream" "foo" {
  name = "SampleLogStream1234"
  log_group_name = "${aws_cloudwatch_log_group.book_log_group.name}"
}
```

Creating alerts is helpful:

```
resource "aws_cloudwatch_metric_alarm" "book_alarm" {
  alarm_name = "book_cpu_alarm"
  comparison_operator = "GreaterThanOrEqualToThreshold"
  evaluation_periods = "2"
  metric_name = "CPUUtilization"
  namespace = "AWS/EC2"
  period = "120"
  statistic = "Average"
  threshold = "80"
  alarm_description = "This metric monitors ec2 cpu utilization"
  insufficient_data_actions = []
}
```

Flow logs

To capture IP traffic for a specific network interface, subnet, or VPC, we need to enable flow logs. They will also go to our CloudWatch log group:

```
resource "aws_iam_role" "test_role" {
  name = "test_role"

  assume_role_policy = <<EOF
{
  "Version": "2012-10-17",
```

```
    "Statement": [
      {
        "Sid": "",
        "Effect": "Allow",
        "Principal": {
          "Service": "vpc-flow-logs.amazonaws.com"
        },
        "Action": "sts:AssumeRole"
      }
    ]
}
EOF
}

resource "aws_iam_role_policy" "test_policy" {
  name = "test_policy"
  role = "${aws_iam_role.test_role.id}"

  policy = <<EOF
{
  "Version": "2012-10-17",
  "Statement": [
    {
      "Action": [
        "logs:CreateLogGroup",
```

```
      ],
      "Effect": "Allow",
      "Resource": "*"
    }
  ]
}
EOF
}
```

> Full version of the preceding code block is available at: `https://github.com/PacktPublishing/Implementing-Cloud-Design-Patterns-for-AWS-Second-Edition`

We will use our captured logs in `Chapter 11`, *Data Processing - Handling Your Data Transformation,* for illustrating data processing patterns.

GuardDuty

To detect unauthorized and unexpected activity in your AWS environment, GuardDuty analyzes and processes data from AWS CloudTrail event logs, VPC Flow Logs, and DNS logs. The logs from these data sources are stored in the Amazon S3 buckets. GuardDuty accesses them there using the HTTPS protocol. While in transit from these data sources to GuardDuty, all of the log data is encrypted. GuardDuty extracts various fields from these logs for profiling and anomaly detection, and then discards the logs. It can also import external datasets:

```
resource "aws_guardduty_detector" "bookdetector" {
  enable = true
}
```

The preceding will create a service account with permissions.

Here is a sample policy:

```
{ "Version": "2012-10-17", "Statement": [ { "Effect": "Allow", "Action": [ "guardduty:*" ], "Resource": "*" }, { "Effect": "Allow", "Action": [ "iam:CreateServiceLinkedRole" ], "Resource": "arn:aws:iam::123456789123:role/aws-service-role/guardduty.amazonaws.com/AWSServiceRoleForAmazonGuardDuty", "Condition": { "StringLike": { "iam:AWSServiceName": "guardduty.amazonaws.com" } } } ] }
```

Vulnerability scanning

Traditional scanning is not really required in the cloud if you follow best practices. Establishing a defense-in-depth posture will frustrate most of the script kiddies. Rotation of sensitive material diminishes the likelihood of an **Advanced Persistent Threat** (**APT**) getting a foothold. However, your product is software and odds are that it uses some open source code (who has time to rewrite everything?). Moving security into the early stages of the SDLC allows us to catch problems before they can be exploited in a production system. We also need to ensure the contents of the Terraform state file are consistent.

Instance-level scanning

We are not huge fans of instance-level scanning, but if you have to do it, AWS Inspector works well. I think that automating updates of your instances when new, patched versions appear is a better way to go. In part two, we'll build out a pipeline to demonstrate this process.

Containers

Workload containerization is also changing the security dynamic. Your product will most likely run in a virtual environment on a minimal, hardened instance in EC2. Chapter 8, *Application Virtualization – Using Cloud Native Patterns for Your Workloads*, will tackle the nuts and bolts of building your containers. I just want to mention here that it is good practice to scan your containers as they are constructed. I like Clair (https://github.com/coreos/clair) as it's easy to plug in to the container registry life cycle workflow.

Code and functions

Moving closer to the code, we recommend scanning your code and functions during the build process. A sample of this pattern, using SonarQube, will be depicted in our continuous delivery chapter.

Buckets

Your objects should be scanned before they get to S3 or onto a persistent disk. However, if you want that extra layer of protection, I like ClamAV. An example of how to compose this pattern in a cloud-friendly way will be presented in the virtualization chapter.

Network

A regular scan of your network is a big part of most compliance programs. The AWS Trusted Advisor service is available to analyze your clouds. As it's currently necessary to code in Java to automate the process, we are going to skip it. It is free and gives you a nice report if you use its console. On the other hand, Nmap (https://nmap.org/) is a great piece of free software for scanning. Used in conjunction with a diff generator, it can easily show you changes in your network. Triggering the scan after a code change offers you immediate feedback on whether any side effects have been introduced. We'll investigate this pattern during our discussion of continuous delivery (as we should always be delivering secure features).

Cloud environment

As your cloud environment grows, sometimes it will be difficult to get a handle on the total attack surface that you oversee. ScoutSuite (`https://github.com/nccgroup/ScoutSuite`), the successor to Scout2, targets the cloud provider's APIs to gather and analyze your environment's configuration data and highlights risk factors, providing a clear view of the attack surface.

Summary

Security vulnerabilities are a fact of life in the cloud world. We have examined a number of practices and patterns for ensuring the integrity and confidentiality of your services. Our discussion focused on defending your assets while they are at rest or on the wire. By reducing exposure to intrusion by establishing our perimeter, we can move on to delivering new features while lessening risk.

The next chapter mainly covers some of the practices that you can use to provide a continuous deployment pipeline.

Further reading

- *AWS: Security Best Practices on AWS* (`https://prod.packtpub.com/in/virtualization-and-cloud/aws-security-best-practices-aws`) provides more detail on what we have done in this chapter
- *Securing Applications on the Cloud* (`https://subscription.packtpub.com/video/virtualization_and_cloud/9781789132717`) will help you get a better understanding of application-level security concerns
- For European GDPR compliance requirement management with AWS, see the video at `https://subscription.packtpub.com/video/business/9781789612530`

Section 2: DevOps Patterns

In this section, you will get your minimum viable product running and prepare for the onslaught of users and their requests for new features. You will also ensure that your customer experience is first class and establish an extensible process for operational engineering.

The following chapters are included in this section:

- Chapter 5, *Continuous Deployment – Introducing New Features with Minimal Risk*
- Chapter 6, *Ephemeral Environments – Sandboxes for Experiments*
- Chapter 7, *Operation and Maintenance – Keeping Things Running at Peak Performance*
- Chapter 8, *Application Virtualization – Using Cloud Native Patterns for Your Workloads*
- Chapter 9, *Antipatterns – Avoiding Counterproductive Solutions*

5
Continuous Deployment - Introducing New Features with Minimal Risk

The aim of deploying your application in a cloud environment is to enable you to put your product in front of your clients quickly and in a reliable and reproducible way, whether this includes new product features, experiments, or configurations. In order to do this, and de-risk shipments, you need to automate the build process, and so you must use continuous deployment. Build processes can take a substantial amount of time, so by using automation, you reduce the amount of repetitive operational work that is required and free up engineering time, which then also allows you to leverage better agile software development practices. This chapter covers some of the practices that you can use to provide a continuous deployment pipeline.

In brief, this chapter will cover the following topics:

- Source control
- CodeBuild
- Testing your code

Technical requirements

The code for this chapter can be found at `https://github.com/PacktPublishing/Implementing-Cloud-Design-Patterns-for-AWS-Second-Edition/tree/master/Chapter03`.

Please use the Cloud9 console to create a directory called `ch5` and change to it before you begin:

```
mkdir ch5 && cd ch5
```

Source control

We have already started along the path to lowering risk by using CodeCommit. Requiring users to authenticate allows us to keep our code private. A remote repository, managed by AWS, provides us with increased availability. Furthermore, the Git commit hash serves as an integrity checksum, ensuring that the data has not been corrupted or altered. Shared source code also improves your ability to deliver new features. So far, our product has mainly focused on infrastructure. As we continue to add new features (or resources, in Terraform speak), the amount of drudgery from typing the same commands over and over increases.

CodeBuild

We will initially use CodeBuild projects to help us automate our Terraform development life cycle. Variables are a construct we have not yet used in our configuration. In your Cloud9 IDE, copy your `main.tf` file from the previous chapter to a new folder called `Chapter5`. Now, let's create a variable file called `tfvars.tf` and add the following information:

```
variable "vpc_id" {
  default = "vpc-1802fb62"
}
variable "aws_public_subnet_id" {
  default = "subnet-476f170d"
}
```

Chapter 5

 Do not put sensitive information in your variables file.

The two variables we created will be used in our next file. In the default VPC, all networks are public. To increase security, we will create a private network for build projects. In a new file called `private.tf`, add the following code:

```
resource "aws_subnet" "cloudpatterns_private" {
  vpc_id = "${var.vpc_id}"
  cidr_block = "172.31.96.0/20"
  map_public_ip_on_launch = false
}

resource "aws_eip" "natgw_eip" {
  vpc = true
}

resource "aws_nat_gateway" "cloudpatterns_nat_gw" {
  allocation_id = "${aws_eip.natgw_eip.id}"
  subnet_id = "${var.aws_public_subnet_id}"
}

resource "aws_route_table" "nat_route_table" {
  vpc_id = "${var.vpc_id}"

  route {
    cidr_block = "0.0.0.0/0"
    gateway_id = "${aws_nat_gateway.cloudpatterns_nat_gw.id}"
  }
}

resource "aws_route_table_association" "a" {
  subnet_id = "${aws_subnet.cloudpatterns_private.id}"
  route_table_id = "${aws_route_table.nat_route_table.id}"
}

resource "aws_security_group" "nat_security_group" {
  name = "allow_all"
  description = "Allow all inbound traffic"
  vpc_id = "${var.vpc_id}"

  ingress {
    from_port = 0
    to_port = 0
    protocol = "-1"
```

```
      cidr_blocks = ["0.0.0.0/0"]
  }

  egress {
    from_port = 0
    to_port = 0
    protocol = "-1"
    cidr_blocks = ["0.0.0.0/0"]
  }
}
```

Go ahead and run your `terraform apply` command (the automation is coming soon, we promise). Let's add some more variables to our `tfvars.tf` file with information you can gather from the last apply:

```
variable "default_security_group_id" {
  default = "sg-0be574956123abb87"
}

variable "aws_codecommit_repository_url" {
  default = "https://git-codecommit.us-east-1.amazonaws.com/v1/repos/cloudpatternsrepo"
}

variable "aws_build_subnet_id" {
  default = ["subnet-034a9e5e46cce777c"]
}
```

Moving towards a model that shares everything requires us to put our Terraform state in a place where it can be accessed by our team. An S3 bucket will work. We can enable versioning on objects so that we have a rollback mechanism in case of a disaster. In a file called `tfstate-bucket.tf`, add the following code:

```
resource "aws_s3_bucket" "cloudpatterns-state" {
  bucket = "cloudpatterns-state"
  acl = "private"

  versioning {
    enabled = true
  }
}
```

Chapter 5

After you apply, exit the AWS console and verify that your bucket is set up correctly:

Terraform uses a remote backend to read and write its state. Now, add the following to the `main.tf` file:

```
terraform {
  backend "s3" {
    bucket = "cloudpatterns-state"
    key = "tfstate"
    region = "us-east-1"
  }
}
```

To have Terraform recognize the new backend, you must Terraform `init && terraform apply`. Your state has now been migrated to the bucket:

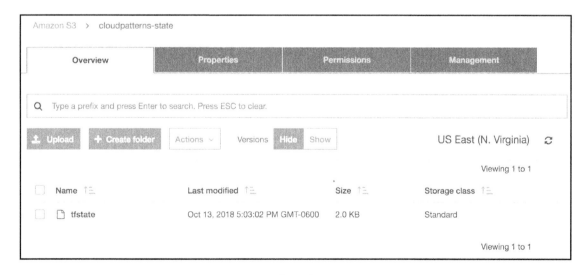

Continuous Deployment - Introducing New Features with Minimal Risk

You can validate whether the object is private by clicking on the **Permissions** tab:

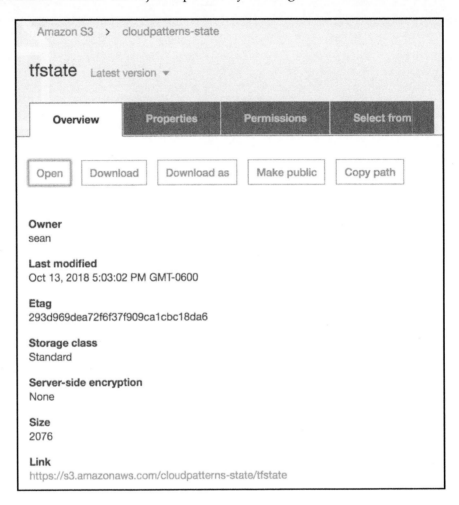

The `tfstate` file can be viewed in the browser:

```
{
    "version": 3,
    "terraform_version": "0.11.7",
    "serial": 2,
    "lineage": "6f99b66f-9d48-5a70-1447-6d4cba21b6dd",
    "modules": [
        {
            "path": [
                "root"
            ],
            "outputs": {},
            "resources": {
                "aws_s3_bucket.cloudpatterns-state": {
                    "type": "aws_s3_bucket",
                    "depends_on": [],
                    "primary": {
                        "id": "cloudpatterns-state",
                        "attributes": {
                            "acceleration_status": "",
                            "acl": "private",
                            "arn": "arn:aws:s3:::cloudpatterns-state",
                            "bucket": "cloudpatterns-state",
                            "bucket_domain_name": "cloudpatterns-state.s3.amazonaws.com",
                            "bucket_regional_domain_name": "cloudpatterns-state.s3.amazonaws.com",
                            "cors_rule.#": "0",
                            "force_destroy": "false",
                            "hosted_zone_id": "Z3AQBSTGFYJSTF",
                            "id": "cloudpatterns-state",
                            "lifecycle_rule.#": "0",
                            "logging.#": "0",
                            "region": "us-east-1",
                            "replication_configuration.#": "0",
                            "request_payer": "BucketOwner",
                            "server_side_encryption_configuration.#": "0",
                            "tags.%": "0",
                            "versioning.#": "1",
                            "versioning.0.enabled": "true",
                            "versioning.0.mfa_delete": "false",
                            "website.#": "0"
                        },
                        "meta": {},
                        "tainted": false
                    },
                    "deposed": [],
                    "provider": "provider.aws"
                }
            },
            "depends_on": []
        }
    ]
}
```

The versions drop-down gives you the option to revert to an older variant of your state. Alternatively, you can download it if needed:

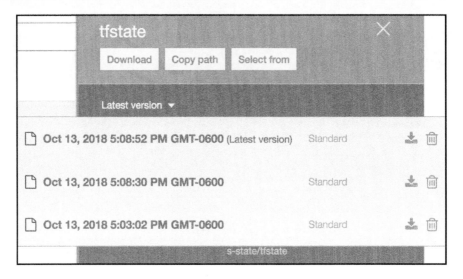

Projects

Now that the prerequisites are in place, we will set up our project. Most of the code is for setting the correct access policies. The good stuff is that all this happens in a container. Since the container cannot get a public IP address, we will put it on the private network we created earlier. Build projects typically produce a deployable artifact. In our case, it will be the Terraform plan file:

```
resource "aws_s3_bucket" "cloudpatterns-codebuild" {
  bucket = "cloudpatterns-codebuild"
  acl = "private"
  versioning {
    enabled = true
  }
}

data "aws_subnet_ids" "example" {
  vpc_id = "${var.vpc_id}"
}

resource "aws_iam_role" "cloudpatterns-codebuild" {
  name = "cloudpatterns-codebuild"

  assume_role_policy = <<EOF
```

```
{
  "Version": "2012-10-17",
  "Statement": [
    {
      "Effect": "Allow",
      "Principal": {
        "Service": "codebuild.amazonaws.com"
      },
      "Action": "sts:AssumeRole"
    }
  ]
}
EOF
}

resource "aws_iam_role_policy" "cloudpatterns-codebuild" {
  role = "${aws_iam_role.cloudpatterns-codebuild.name}"

  policy = <<POLICY
{
  "Version": "2012-10-17",
  "Statement": [
    {
      "Effect": "Allow",
      "Resource": [
        "*"
      ],
      "Action": [
        "logs:CreateLogGroup",
        "logs:CreateLogStream",
        "logs:PutLogEvents"
      ]
    },
    {
      "Effect": "Allow",
      "Action": [
        "ec2:*"
      ],
      "Resource": "*"
    },
    {
      "Effect": "Allow",
      "Action": [
        "codecommit:*"
      ],
      "Resource": "*"
    },
    {
```

```
      "Effect": "Allow",
      "Action": [
        "s3:*"
      ],
      "Resource": [
        "${aws_s3_bucket.cloudpatterns-codebuild.arn}",
        "${aws_s3_bucket.cloudpatterns-codebuild.arn}/*"
      ]
    }
  ]
}
POLICY
}

resource "aws_codebuild_project" "cloudpatterns-codebuild" {
  name = "cloudpatterns-project"
  description = "cloudpatterns_codebuild_project"
  build_timeout = "5"
  service_role = "${aws_iam_role.cloudpatterns-codebuild.arn}"

  artifacts {
    type = "S3"
    location = "${aws_s3_bucket.cloudpatterns-codebuild.bucket}"
  }

/* cache {
    type = "S3"
    location = "${aws_s3_bucket.cloudpatterns-codebuild.bucket}"
  } */

  environment {
    compute_type = "BUILD_GENERAL1_SMALL"
    image = "aws/codebuild/ubuntu-base:14.04"
    type = "LINUX_CONTAINER"
  }

  source {
    type = "CODECOMMIT"
    location = "${var.aws_codecommit_repository_url}"
    git_clone_depth = 1
  }

  vpc_config {
    vpc_id = "${var.vpc_id}"

    subnets = [
      "${var.aws_build_subnet_id}",
    ]
```

```
    security_group_ids = [
      "${var.default_security_group_id}",
    ]
  }

  tags {
    "Environment" = "cloudpatterns"
  }
}
```

After you apply, you can see your project in the Amazon console:

The project uses a `YAML` file as a build template. Let's go to the root of our repository and create one. The default name is `buildspec.yml`:

```
version: 0.2
# adapted from
https://github.com/cloudreach/awsloft-terraform-ci/blob/master/buildspec-dev.yml
# and
https://stackoverflow.com/questions/44005005/aws-codebuild-terraform-provider

env:
  variables:
    TF_VERSION: "0.11.10"
phases:

  install:
    commands:
      - cd /usr/bin
      - curl -s -qL -o terraform.zip https://releases.hashicorp.com/terraform/0.11.10/terraform_0.11.10_linux_amd64.zip
      - unzip -o terraform.zip

  build:
    commands:
      - echo "changing directory to $CODEBUILD_SRC_DIR"
```

```
      - cd $CODEBUILD_SRC_DIR/Chapter5/
      - terraform init
      - terraform plan -no-color -out cloudpatterns.tfplan

  post_build:
    commands:
      - echo "terraform plan completed on `date`"


artifacts:
  files:
    - '**/*'
```

Select the project and start your build. Accept all the defaults:

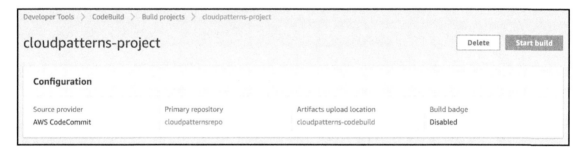

The project will pull our source from CodeCommit, initialize Terraform, run the plan, and then copy it into our bucket. Containers are so excellent. Let's create a Lambda function to run the apply.

Event-driven architecture

What we need first is some code to install Terraform, get our plan, and apply it. Open up a new file, paste in the following code, and save it as `terraform.py`:

```
# -*- coding: utf-8 -*-
# adapted from https://github.com/FitnessKeeper/terraform-lambda

import os
import subprocess
import urllib
import boto3

# Version of Terraform that we're using
TERRAFORM_VERSION = '0.11.11'
```

```python
# Download URL for Terraform
TERRAFORM_DOWNLOAD_URL = (
'https://releases.hashicorp.com/terraform/%s/terraform_%s_linux_amd64.zip'
    % (TERRAFORM_VERSION, TERRAFORM_VERSION))

# Paths where Terraform should be installed
TERRAFORM_DIR = os.path.join('/tmp', 'terraform_%s' % TERRAFORM_VERSION)
TERRAFORM_PATH = os.path.join(TERRAFORM_DIR, 'terraform')

def check_call(args):
    """Wrapper for subprocess that checks if a process runs correctly,
    and if not, prints stdout and stderr.
    """
    proc = subprocess.Popen(args,
        stdout=subprocess.PIPE,
        stderr=subprocess.PIPE,
        cwd='/tmp')
    stdout, stderr = proc.communicate()
    if proc.returncode != 0:
        print(stdout)
        print(stderr)
        raise subprocess.CalledProcessError(
            returncode=proc.returncode,
            cmd=args)

def install_terraform():
    """Install Terraform on the Lambda instance."""
    # Most of a Lambda's disk is read-only, but some transient storage is
    # provided in /tmp, so we install Terraform here. This storage may
    # persist between invocations, so we skip downloading a new version if
    # it already exists.
    # http://docs.aws.amazon.com/lambda/latest/dg/lambda-introduction.html
    if os.path.exists(TERRAFORM_PATH):
        return

    urllib.urlretrieve(TERRAFORM_DOWNLOAD_URL, '/tmp/terraform.zip')

    # Flags:
    # '-o' = overwrite existing files without prompting
    # '-d' = output directory
    check_call(['unzip', '-o', '/tmp/terraform.zip', '-d', TERRAFORM_DIR])

    check_call([TERRAFORM_PATH, '--version'])


def apply_terraform_plan(s3_bucket, path):
    """Download a Terraform plan from S3 and run a 'terraform apply'.
```

```
        :param s3_bucket: Name of the S3 bucket where the plan is stored.
        :param path: Path to the Terraform planfile in the S3 bucket.
        """
        # Although the /tmp directory may persist between invocations, we always
        # download a new copy of the planfile, as it may have changed externally.
        s3 = boto3.resource('s3')
        planfile = s3.Object(s3_bucket, path)
        planfile.download_file('/tmp/terraform.plan')
        check_call([TERRAFORM_PATH, 'apply', '/tmp/terraform.plan'])

def handler(event, context):
        s3_bucket = event['Records'][0]['s3']['bucket']['name']
        path = event['Records'][0]['s3']['object']['key']

        install_terraform()
        apply_terraform_plan(s3_bucket=s3_bucket, path=path)
```

Lambda expects a bundle of code to be provided. We'll zip up our file by using the following command:

```
zip cloudpatterns_lambda.zip terraform.py
```

Now, we need to create our function with Terraform. In Cloud9, compose `lambda_terraform.tf` by using the following code:

```
resource "aws_iam_role" "iam_for_lambda" {
  name = "iam_for_lambda"

  assume_role_policy = <<EOF
{
  "Version": "2012-10-17",
  "Statement": [
    {
      "Action": "sts:AssumeRole",
      "Principal": {
        "Service": "lambda.amazonaws.com"
      },
      "Effect": "Allow"
    },
    {
      "Sid": "",
      "Effect": "Allow",
      "Principal": {
        "Service": "cloudtrail.amazonaws.com"
      },
      "Action": "sts:AssumeRole"
```

```
      }
    ]
}
EOF
}

resource "aws_lambda_permission" "allow_bucket" {
  statement_id = "AllowExecutionFromS3Bucket"
  action = "lambda:InvokeFunction"
  function_name =
"${aws_lambda_function.cloudpatterns_terraform_lambda.arn}"
  principal = "s3.amazonaws.com"
  source_arn = "${aws_s3_bucket.cloudpatterns-codebuild.arn}"
}

resource "aws_lambda_function" "cloudpatterns_terraform_lambda" {
  filename = "cloudpatterns_lambda.zip"
  function_name = "cloudpatterns_terraform_lambda"
  role = "${aws_iam_role.iam_for_lambda.arn}"
  handler = "terraform.handler"
  runtime = "python3.7"
  source_code_hash = "${base64sha256(file("cloudpatterns_lambda.zip"))}"

  environment {
    variables = {
      production = "false"
    }
  }
}

resource "aws_s3_bucket_notification" "bucket_notification" {
  bucket = "${aws_s3_bucket.cloudpatterns-codebuild.id}"

  lambda_function {
    lambda_function_arn =
"${aws_lambda_function.cloudpatterns_terraform_lambda.arn}"
    events = ["s3:ObjectCreated:*"]
    filter_suffix = ".tfplan"
  }
}
```

The **Lambda** dashboard should show your function after another apply:

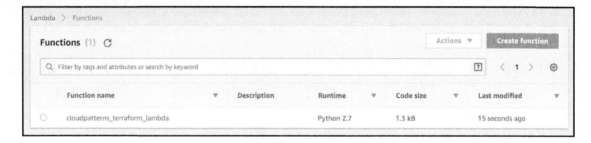

The function we created is designed to be triggered by the creation of any object with the suffix `tfplan` in our bucket. Go ahead and run `terraform plan-no-color-out cloudpatterns.tfplan`. Push the new file up to S3 using the GUI:

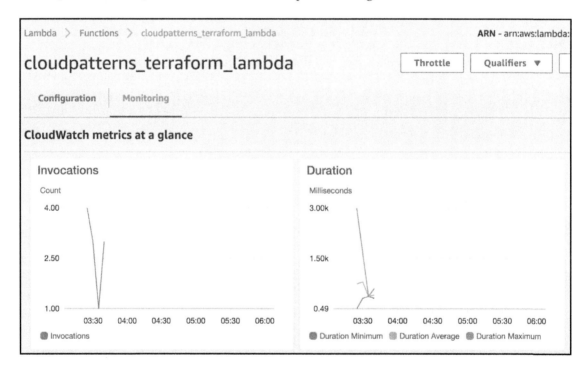

You can verify that your Lambda has run and see some metrics in the **Monitoring** tab after you select the **Functions** in the console.

Build servers

There are many organizations that want to keep control of the application build and deployment steps, separate from the deployment environment. There are many tools that can help with this, but the two most well-known are Jenkins and Atlassian Bamboo. These tools are used to manage the build pipeline, pulling together the software build, automated testing, environment build, and deployment strategies to be *all under one roof.*

Testing your code

Best practices for software development include testing your code. We have been testing whether Terraform is delivering the required outputs by validating that our resources exist in the AWS console. The automation of tests gives us a repeatable way to confirm that our product is behaving in the expected way. However, it is important to test non-functional requirements as well. Product security and availability are two aspects that affect every task. In addition to reducing toil through continuous builds and deployment of our code, we must ensure code quality. To this effect, we will create another CodeBuild project using the open source Sonar (https://www.sonarqube.org/) project.

 You need to create an account at SonarCloud to get the variables for your build.

We will start by creating a `sonarqube.yml` file in our root directory:

```
version: 0.2

phases:
  install:
    commands:
      - wget https://binaries.sonarsource.com/Distribution/sonar-scanner-cli/sonar-scanner-cli-3.2.0.1227-linux.zip
      - unzip sonar-scanner-cli-3.2.0.1227-linux.zip
      - export PATH=$PATH:./sonar-scanner-3.2.0.1227-linux/bin/
  build:
    commands:
      - sonar-scanner -Dsonar.projectKey=<yourProjectKey> -Dsonar.organization=<your-org> -Dsonar.sources=. -Dsonar.host.url=https://sonarcloud.io -Dsonar.login=<yourToken>
```

Reusing code is another benefit of a good SDLC, but now is not the time for it. Let's copy the preceding `codebuild.tf` project resource into `codetest.tf`. Change the following sections:

```
resource "aws_codebuild_project" "cloudpatterns-codetest" {
  name = "cloudpatterns-test-project"
  description = "cloudpatterns_codetest_project"
  ...
  source {
    type = "CODECOMMIT"
    location = "${var.aws_codecommit_repository_url}"
    ...
    git_clone_depth = 1
    buildspec = "sonarqube.yml"
  }
  ...
}
```

Apply and run the **Build logs** from the console. You will see that they all pass:

Name	Status	Context	Duration	Start time	End time
SUBMITTED	Succeeded	-	<1 sec	Oct 14, 2018 10:13 PM	Oct 14, 2018 10:13 PM
PROVISIONING	Succeeded	-	18 secs	Oct 14, 2018 10:13 PM	Oct 14, 2018 10:13 PM
DOWNLOAD_SOURCE	Succeeded	-	10 secs	Oct 14, 2018 10:13 PM	Oct 14, 2018 10:13 PM
INSTALL	Succeeded	-	8 secs	Oct 14, 2018 10:13 PM	Oct 14, 2018 10:13 PM
PRE_BUILD	Succeeded	-	<1 sec	Oct 14, 2018 10:13 PM	Oct 14, 2018 10:13 PM
BUILD	Succeeded	-	34 secs	Oct 14, 2018 10:13 PM	Oct 14, 2018 10:14 PM
POST_BUILD	Succeeded	-	<1 sec	Oct 14, 2018 10:14 PM	Oct 14, 2018 10:14 PM
UPLOAD_ARTIFACTS	Succeeded	-	<1 sec	Oct 14, 2018 10:14 PM	Oct 14, 2018 10:14 PM
FINALIZING	Succeeded	-	2 secs	Oct 14, 2018 10:14 PM	Oct 14, 2018 10:14 PM
COMPLETED	Succeeded	-	-	Oct 14, 2018 10:14 PM	-

You should see build logs similar to the following. These are also available in CloudWatch for further analysis:

```
[Container] 2018/10/15 04:13:26 Waiting for agent ping
[Container] 2018/10/15 04:13:29 Waiting for DOWNLOAD_SOURCE
[Container] 2018/10/15 04:13:40 Phase is DOWNLOAD_SOURCE
[Container] 2018/10/15 04:13:40
```

```
CODEBUILD_SRC_DIR=/codebuild/output/src069182567/src/git-codecommit.us-
east-1.amazonaws.com/v1/repos/cloudpatternsrepo
[Container] 2018/10/15 04:13:40 YAML location is
/codebuild/output/src069182567/src/git-codecommit.us-
east-1.amazonaws.com/v1/repos/cloudpatternsrepo/sonarqube.yml
[Container] 2018/10/15 04:13:40 Processing environment variables
[Container] 2018/10/15 04:13:40 Moving to directory
/codebuild/output/src069182567/src/git-codecommit.us-
east-1.amazonaws.com/v1/repos/cloudpatternsrepo
[Container] 2018/10/15 04:13:40 Registering with agent
[Container] 2018/10/15 04:13:40 Phases found in YAML: 2
[Container] 2018/10/15 04:13:40 BUILD: 1 commands
[Container] 2018/10/15 04:13:40 INSTALL: 3 commands
[Container] 2018/10/15 04:13:40 Phase complete: DOWNLOAD_SOURCE Success:
true
[Container] 2018/10/15 04:13:40 Phase context status code: Message:
[Container] 2018/10/15 04:13:40 Entering phase INSTALL
[Container] 2018/10/15 04:13:40 Running command wget
https://binaries.sonarsource.com/Distribution/sonar-scanner-cli/sonar-scann
er-cli-3.2.0.1227-linux.zip
--2018-10-15 04:13:40--
https://binaries.sonarsource.com/Distribution/sonar-scanner-cli/sonar-scann
er-cli-3.2.0.1227-linux.zip
Resolving binaries.sonarsource.com (binaries.sonarsource.com)...
91.134.125.245
Connecting to binaries.sonarsource.com
(binaries.sonarsource.com)|91.134.125.245|:443... connected.
HTTP request sent, awaiting response... 200 OK
Length: 73847400 (70M) [application/zip]
Saving to: 'sonar-scanner-cli-3.2.0.1227-linux.zip'

0K .......... .......... .......... .......... .......... 0% 257K 4m40s
50K .......... .......... .......... .......... .......... 0% 516K 3m30s
...
72100K .......... ...... 100% 206M=3.1s

2018-10-15 04:13:44 (22.8 MB/s) - 'sonar-scanner-cli-3.2.0.1227-linux.zip'
saved [73847400/73847400]

[Container] 2018/10/15 04:13:45 Running command unzip sonar-scanner-
cli-3.2.0.1227-linux.zip
Archive: sonar-scanner-cli-3.2.0.1227-linux.zip
creating: sonar-scanner-3.2.0.1227-linux/
...
inflating: sonar-scanner-3.2.0.1227-linux/bin/sonar-scanner-debug
finishing deferred symbolic links:
sonar-scanner-3.2.0.1227-linux/jre/lib/amd64/server/libjsig.so ->
../libjsig.so
```

```
[Container] 2018/10/15 04:13:48 Running command export PATH=$PATH:./sonar-
scanner-3.2.0.1227-linux/bin/

[Container] 2018/10/15 04:13:48 Phase complete: INSTALL Success: true
[Container] 2018/10/15 04:13:48 Phase context status code: Message:
[Container] 2018/10/15 04:13:48 Entering phase PRE_BUILD
[Container] 2018/10/15 04:13:48 Phase complete: PRE_BUILD Success: true
[Container] 2018/10/15 04:13:48 Phase context status code: Message:
[Container] 2018/10/15 04:13:48 Entering phase BUILD
[Container] 2018/10/15 04:13:48 Running command sonar-scanner -
Dsonar.projectKey=cure51-gapes -Dsonar.organization=skibum55-github -
Dsonar.sources=. -Dsonar.host.url=https://sonarcloud.io -
Dsonar.login=b85ce42d96cc973761366dfbeeb8ede60cc0ab4f
INFO: Scanner configuration file: /codebuild/output/src069182567/src/git-
codecommit.us-east-1.amazonaws.com/v1/repos/cloudpatternsrepo/sonar-
scanner-3.2.0.1227-linux/conf/sonar-scanner.properties
INFO: Project root configuration file: NONE
INFO: SonarQube Scanner 3.2.0.1227
...
INFO: ANALYSIS SUCCESSFUL, you can browse
https://sonarcloud.io/dashboard?id=cure51-gapes
INFO: Note that you will be able to access the updated dashboard once the
server has processed the submitted analysis report
INFO: More about the report processing at
https://sonarcloud.io/api/ce/task?id=AWZ17plzny3k_lyf1dFM
INFO: Task total time: 10.111 s
INFO: ------------------------------------------------------------------
---
INFO: EXECUTION SUCCESS
INFO: ------------------------------------------------------------------
---
INFO: Total time: 34.054s
INFO: Final Memory: 30M/315M
INFO: ------------------------------------------------------------------
---

[Container] 2018/10/15 04:14:23 Phase complete: BUILD Success: true
[Container] 2018/10/15 04:14:23 Phase context status code: Message:
[Container] 2018/10/15 04:14:23 Entering phase POST_BUILD
[Container] 2018/10/15 04:14:23 Phase complete: POST_BUILD Success: true
```

Chapter 5

Your public products report is now available on SonarCloud:

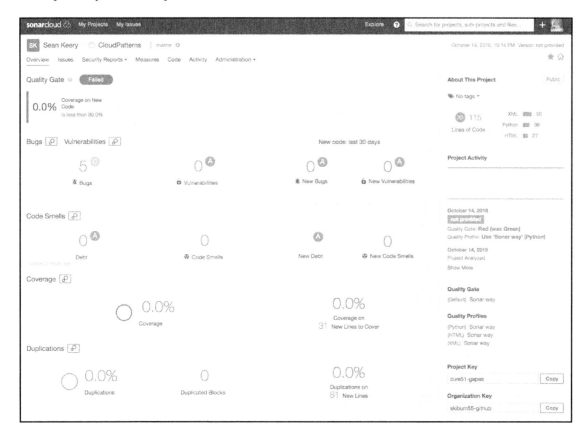

That isn't very good. But don't despair. SonarCloud does not really understand Terraform. If you are developing using Java, .NET, or Python, your results will be much more pertinent. In the next chapter, we will go into more depth on some of the short-lived resources we took advantage of in our continuous delivery efforts.

Summary

In this chapter, we've covered more on how to construct a build pipeline for AWS deployments. We've discussed how to manage code and source control, how to set off a build, and how to set up some basic testing. We've also briefly mentioned some alternatives. As with all things, there are a myriad of ways of achieving the same thing; it's up to you and your organization to determine which is best for you. In the next chapter, we will supply a design pattern to aid you in your move to the cloud. The financial benefits, the advantages for your customers, and the improved velocity of your software engineers will be considered.

Further reading

- Information about Jenkins: `https://jenkins.io`
- Information about Atlassian Bamboo: `https://www.atlassian.com/software/bamboo`

6
Ephemeral Environments - Sandboxes for Experiments

In this chapter, we will supply additional design patterns to aid in your success in using the cloud services. The financial benefits, the advantages for your customers, and the improved velocity of your software engineers will be considered. Throughout this book, we have already covered many patterns that can be applied to different use cases, but are flexible in many ways. They can be mixed and matched, and even stacked to create very cool setups. This is only one piece of the much larger puzzle, however, of getting into the cloud mindset.

In brief, we will cover the following topics in this chapter:

- Developer productivity
- Exploring deployment strategies
- Facilitating self-service
- Using multiple environments
- Testing your environment

Developer productivity

In the previous chapter, we saw the power of cloud computing in our continuous delivery processes. Short-lived containers and functions provided on-demand computing for our build and test phases. By applying these principles to all aspects of our product, we can deliver a secure, globally available product at minimal cost.

Ephemeral Environments - Sandboxes for Experiments

Our Cloud9 workspace has given us a complete web-based development environment. Let's look at the benefits of enabling the session to be shared between developers:

- The ability to remotely pair with another developer helps us move our traditional quality assurance practices to the beginning of the development cycle.
- Catching bugs before they get into running software reduces our cost sixfold.
- Our integrations with CodeBuild and Lambda add a level of consistency to the construction of our artifacts.
- Component reuse practices will help us avoid downstream software incompatibilities.

The base Ubuntu container we used for our plan can be also be reused to mimic our production environment as often as we would like. Runtime variable insertion allows us to use the same code to build many VPCs. Terraform supports overriding configuration at runtime. Our container runtime also allows us to insert environment variables at startup.

In addition to long-running containers, which will be covered in `Chapter 8`, *Application Virtualization - Using Cloud Native Patterns for Your Workloads*, **Amazon Web Services** (**AWS**) offers us virtual desktops. For traditional Microsoft Windows product development, these instances allow us to persist with a heavier-weight user experience. Small businesses can also, if necessary, take advantage of this offering to reduce their support and maintenance costs. Large enterprises can enforce their policies to remote workers and improve the speed of their patching and upgrade cycles.

Exploring deployment strategies

Traditionally, deployment of software was a rare event. Every year, you would take all the new product features, bundle them up, and install them on your servers. The tightly coupled features of your monolith introduced a great deal of risk. If there was a single fault in your code, it could cause cascading failures in your product. Modern cloud development practices recommend decomposing your software. We have followed this pattern by creating separate files for unrelated Terraform resources. Segmenting our content even more would have given us additional benefits, but we are striving for a minimal viable product (optimization will come later).

In our case, deploying immediately to a production environment could have impacts on our product's service level agreements. Cycling our WordPress instances at the same time would reduce availability as we couldn't guarantee the sequence of events. A better strategy would be to take our east instance down first, upgrade or install our product, then rebuild our west instance after our load balancer reports that east is healthy.

This pattern is called a blue-green deployment. Variations include a red-black, where a new set of instances is created and mapped to a pool. The load balancer pool is then re-targeted at the new group, which accepts all traffic. Rolling back from a failed deployment just requires you to revert your load balancer changes. The blue-green avoids total system downtime at the cost of availability. Half of your capacity is offline at once, increasing risk in the case of an unexpected traffic surge.

A better strategy involves combining the preceding patterns. This practice is called canarying. New instances are brought up and slowly added to the production pool. As performance of the new software is validated against historical data, the old instances are retired. The **automated canary analysis** (**ACA**) pattern decreases risk when introducing complex distributed systems. And our systems do get more complicated as we move further up the stack. `Chapter 8`, *Application Virtualization - Using Cloud Native Patterns for Your Workloads*, touches on the benefits of doing this, but we need to understand how microservices require us to do thorough testing before deployment in order to avoid upstream consequences.

Facilitating self-service

To increase developer productivity, we must allow our team to experiment with new services and functionality with AWS. AWS releases new features at a rate that makes it hard for security personnel to review. We need to trust our developers in order for them to grow. A low-trust workplace is usually a high-turnover one. Isolated VPCs let developers play as needed while containing any ill-conceived experiments. Letting developers have their own playground is a great practice and will be expanded on in the next section.

Templates

Amazon and its partners provide a great deal of expertise that we can leverage in their services. CloudFormation templates and Lightsail let you build on known good configurations. Terraform does not provide a comprehensive API for Lightsail because many of the ingredients it uses are standard AWS parts. However, for developers unfamiliar with the infrastructure as code paradigm, it is a good place to get started. Whereas the standard AWS console lists nearly 100 services, Lightsail reduces this to five concepts as:

- Instances
- Databases
- Networking
- Storage
- Snapshots

For developers just getting started on AWS, we recommend playing around in Lightsail in order to familiarize yourselves with the basics.

CloudFormation can take us to the next level. Stacks are its key construct. They work in a very similar fashion to Terraform. We feel that they are complementary technologies. Terraform can create a stack resource. Vendors that are unable to provide a simple, single-instance application, such as our Bitnami WordPress, provide CloudFormation templates to deploy their systems. As you can see with this MongoDB quickstart example (`https://aws.amazon.com/quickstart/architecture/mongodb/`), the architectures can take advantage of many of the availability and security features we have discussed previously.

To deploy this entire stack is quite simple with Terraform. Copy your `main.tf` file from the previous chapter, rename your `state` file and initialize before you apply.

```
resource "aws_cloudformation_stack" "mongo" {
  name = "mongo-stack"
  template_url =
"https://github.com/aws-quickstart/quickstart-mongodb/blob/master/templates/mongodb.template"
}
```

That is a pretty easy way to get it done.

> More details on available templates can be found at `https://aws.amazon.com/cloudformation/aws-cloudformation-templates/`.

Using multiple environments

To minimize risk during our deployments, we can create our product in a non-production environment. In our case, we will designate the AWS west region as our test location. A common practice for tiered environments includes development, testing, staging, and production. Everything below, or to the left of, production is grouped as non-production. Often there is considerable overlap in the functionality of the environments and in many organizations; they exist within the same cloud.

Our goal is to have non-production environments that have parity with production. However, as we discussed earlier, our service levels do not need to be as high in some non-production aspects. Since our data is not real, consistency is a less important piece of the puzzle for developers in their environment, whereas the test environments may need a truly durable environment to run stress tests on your systems.

Staging may be done within production if your deployment strategies allow you to isolate product versions from your customer. By identifying our customers, we can define SLOs for all our environments. In our product, developers will need a high availability from the AWS APIs, but are less concerned about the response time. End users need both.

A product mindset requires us to be in constant contact with all of the users, to regularly gather feedback on existing systems. We must always strive to identify new features that will improve the developers productivity or optimize our costs. Balancing those features with our need for isolation of workloads gives us the mix of environments that works for us.

Testing your environment

As we move workloads to the cloud, we have the benefit of nearly unlimited capacity. In Chapter 3, *Availability Patterns - Understanding Your Needs*, we looked into how we could create an auto-scaling group. The resource we created used Spot Instances, a low-cost ephemeral compute capacity, to increase our number of instances:

```
scaling_adjustment = 4
  adjustment_type = "ChangeInCapacity"
```

In the *Persistence Patterns* section of the book, we will dive into how to use our AWS metrics to choose what to measure. For now, we need to understand that whatever we choose as our default will at some point be suboptimal. Odds are that it will be on initial creation. We must constantly be validating our assumptions about what we've built.

Ephemeral Environments - Sandboxes for Experiments

Load testing with real data is one of the best ways to substantiate we are moving in the right direction with our postulations. Our infrastructure-as-code solution provides a reproducible way to rebuild our entire product in another region or availability zone for this purpose. We will leave the test environment setup to you and look at an easy way to test the effectiveness of your auto-scaling from Cloud9. Python will be our language du jour again for this example. Locust.io (https://github.com/locustio/locust) equips us with a scalable load testing framework:

1. We will install locust from the command line first:

   ```
   sudo python -m pip install locustio
   ```

2. The password for our WordPress is generated on first boot (security!). We can get it through the AWS CLI:

   ```
   aws ec2 get-console-output --instance-id i-1234567890abcdef0 |grep 'setting bitnami application password to'
   ```

3. Create a new file called `locustfile.py` in your `Chapter 6` folder:

   ```
   from locust import HttpLocust, TaskSet, task

   class UserBehavior(TaskSet):
       def on_start(self):
           self.login()

       def on_stop(self):

       def login(self):
           self.client.post("/wp-admin", {"username":"user", "password":"reading"})

       def logout(self):
           self.client.post("/logout", {"username":"user", "password":"reading"})

       @task(1)
       def profile(self):
           self.client.get("/profile")

   class WebsiteUser(HttpLocust):
       task_set = UserBehavior
       min_wait = 5000
       max_wait = 9000
   ```

4. Run the preceding file using the following command:

   ```
   locust --host=https://www.book.cloudpatterns.uk --no-web -c 1000 -r 100
   ```

   You should see some results like this:

   ```
   Name # reqs # fails Avg Min Max | Median req/s
   --------------------------------------------------------------------------
   GET // 2739 0(0.00%) 16 4 360 | 8 95.10
   POST //logout 0 1000(100.00%) 0 0 0 | 0 0.00
   GET //profile 1424 0(0.00%) 15 4 289 | 8 48.60
   POST //wp-admin 0 1000(100.00%) 0 0 0 | 0 0.00
   --------------------------------------------------------------------------
   Total 4163 2000(48.04%) 143.70

   Percentage of the requests completed within given times
    Name # reqs 50% 66% 75% 80% 90% 95% 98% 99% 100%
   --------------------------------------------------------------------------
   GET // 2739 8 10 11 12 15 34 200 230 360
   GET //profile 1424 8 10 11 12 15 26 160 220 290
   --------------------------------------------------------------------------
   Total 4163 8 10 11 12 15 31 190 230 360

   Error report
    # occurrences Error
   --------------------------------------------------------------------------
    1000 POST //wp-admin: "HTTPError(u'405 Client Error: Method Not Allowed for url: http://axontrader.cfapps.io//wp-admin',)"
    1000 POST //logout: "HTTPError(u'405 Client Error: Method Not Allowed for url: http://axontrader.cfapps.io//logout',)"
   --------------------------------------------------------------------------
   ```

Ephemeral Environments - Sandboxes for Experiments

5. Go to the AWS console and select your instance. At the bottom of the screen, select the **Monitoring** tab. Since we are not paying for higher resolution, our statistics may take a moment to come through (low SLA). Eventually, you will see a graph representing the load we flung at our instance:

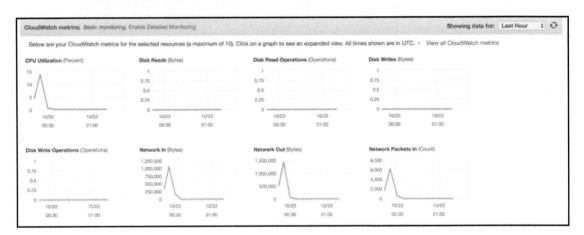

At some point, our instance became overloaded and triggered the auto-scaling group to add capacity. We will overwhelm our C9 instance before the web server is at capacity. However, after our synthetic traffic decreases, the excess auto-scaling capacity will be released.

Other options for testing in your production environment include using a second set of ELBs, perhaps internal to your VPC, to just take requests from a CodeBuild project. Some new features of Kubernetes allow you to mirror your production traffic to your product release candidates. This allows you to identify anomalies before you shift any routes.

Managing cost

We fabricated a workload equivalent to 10,000 users. Using our existing C9 instance didn't add a thing to our bill. A Spot Instance came online for a few minutes. It cost 10 cents. That has zero impact on our production east traffic. Pretty sweet! Let's look at our billing page. Oh wait, we don't have access, so let's create that access:

1. Create `billingIAM.tf` as follows:

```
resource "aws_iam_group_policy_attachment" "test-attach" {
  group      = "${aws_iam_group.billpayers.name}"
  policy_arn = "arn:aws:iam::aws:policy/job-function/Billing"
```

Chapter 6

```
}

resource "aws_iam_group" "billpayers" {
  name = "billpayers"
  path = "/users/"
}

resource "aws_iam_group_membership" "billinggroup" {
  name = "billing-group-membership"

  users = [
    "cloudpatterns",
  ]

  group = "${aws_iam_group.billpayers.name}"
}
```

That totally did not work. Apparently, the root user needs to enable IAM billing access. That makes sense. We can do that in the GUI.

2. Click on **My Account** and go to the section entitled **IAM User and Role Access to Billing Information**. Check the box and click **Update**:

[119]

Now you can see the billing pages:

We've spent about $30 on our product so far. Not bad for a pretty secure, distributed, highly available system.

Summary

In this chapter, we discussed some high-level topics that are making headlines in the DevOps movement and can improve our productivity within AWS. We touched on using temporary development environments and discussed how tools such as Terraform and CloudFormation allow us to create short-lived playgrounds for developers. Finally, we discussed how we can optimize our testing and deployment to make use of the flexibility of the cloud and AWS. The next chapter will be combine various processes that will help you to deliver a product with high availability and ensure that, in the case of a disaster, you have practiced your recovery methods.

Exercises

1. Use resource tags to clean up your environment with a Lambda in the case of a lost `tfstate`.
2. Set up a multinode locust cluster using Terraform to simulate more users.
3. Validate that your autoscaler worked when CPU hit 45%.
4. Deny access to all users to the AWS billing resources.

7
Operation and Maintenance - Keeping Things Running at Peak Performance

In this chapter, we will provide examples of patterns for the care and running of your product. Service levels and their components will be introduced. Practices leading to shortened feedback loops and increased cooperation will be emphasized. The designing of reusable templates, configurations, and processes will be included. Our focus on API-driven automation will continue to be highlighted.

We will cover the following topics in this chapter:

- Desilofication
- Measurement
- Fault injection
- Business continuity
- Reduction

Technical requirements

The code for this chapter can be found at `https://github.com/PacktPublishing/Implementing-Cloud-Design-Patterns-for-AWS-Second-Edition/ch7`.

Please use the Cloud9 console to create a directory called `ch4` and change to it before you begin:

```
mkdir ch7 && cd ch7
```

Desilofication

The cloud is all about breaking down patterns that have solidified in traditional enterprises. Specialization has reinforced these practices. A networking expert in a siloed organization often does not have to care about how their design affects the paying customer. This occurs because that professional is seeing a blinkered view of their clients.

As we create or move workloads to the cloud, we have the opportunity to demolish these standalone knowledge depots. Desilofication is the process of breaking down barriers to knowledge caused by separate organizations not cooperating or being aware of the other's existence.

Product mindset

Our product mindset encourages us to seek out and understand the business outcomes of our users. Understanding that our instances must have an IP address doesn't really tell us anything about business value. Knowing that all credit card transactions need to be approved, or denied, in under three seconds provides us with a lot more context.

The difference between the two previous examples is in a project versus product mindset. Projects are short-term delivery efforts. They do not encompass the continued operations and evolution of a product. Products may live on for many years if they continue to be of use to customers.

Balanced team

Products are most successful when they are handled by a balanced team. We have at engineering practices in previous chapters. This is because we treat our obstacles as problems and look for a solution. An engineer is a critical representative of the cloud team. The **Product Manager (PM)** is probably a new member of your team. They are responsible for understanding the needs of the customers (hopefully, you have more than one). As the customer base grows, they also need to prioritize new features.

There is a cyclical nature between the PM and engineers on the cloud team. Engineers work with the PM to estimate the effort required to create or modify aspects of the work. The engineers also pair with the PM to understand when an MVP has reached its limits. Typically, at this point, instead of working on new items, engineers should be assigned to reduce technical debt in order to improve reliability. Not to say that this always happens, but that is the ideal.

User-centered design

Every feature you are working on should add value for the product users. We recommend a process that defines personas for each category of users. Write feature stories that revolve around what people want and why it's important. Acceptance criteria should define usability goals as well as functionality. Strive to create short feedback cycles, iterative design, and write tests before the code.

Self-service

A huge benefit of the cloud is the ability to let your users get what they need quickly. Allowing your services to be consumed quickly and easily, in a safe setting, encourages experimentation among the team. Amazon's barrier to entry is low and your product should follow their lead. Sketch out your existing workflows to see where potential bottlenecks exist. Keep track of which services your customers are using. Remove features that aren't adding value.

Measurement

For our product to thrive, we must measure for success, as shown in the following examples:

- The number of new features released in a week is a good user-facing metric
- Requests that took over 200 ms to provide a response is an important metric for the engineers running your services
- Dollars spent on your site by customers is a crucial business dimension to review

In the previous chapter, we introduced rules that would trigger an event to enlarge our instance pool. Now, we will dig into the components of that method to better understand why this pattern is so important in the cloud.

Indicators

To demonstrate that we are accomplishing the right thing, we must identify signals that show what we are doing. These indicators are crucial to prove our hypotheses have been validated. The best indicators are a ratio of two metrics. An example could be the number of good responses divided by the total number of responses. This is a big change from traditional threshold-based metrics. In a cloud-based environment, appropriate metrics will not need to be updated when an auto scaling event takes place. Those events may be driven by more conventional dimensions such as CPU consumption or free memory, but they are not necessarily important to product success. In `Chapter 12`, *Observability – Understanding How Your Products Are Behaving*, we will consider how reliability engineers can deluged by meaningless alerts if indicators are inappropriately configured.

> The golden signals (`https://landing.google.com/sre/sre-book/chapters/monitoring-distributed-systems/`) are a good starting point for any service.

Objectives

One hundred percent is not the right objective, whatever your indicator may be. You will have outages. AWS will have downtime. Hackers might try to penetrate your awesome security. The chaos army could target you! Architecting your services according to the patterns presented in this book will help to minimize the effects of interruptions on your business. Anyway, the cost of 100% uptime is prohibitive. So, set some realistic targets and work from there. Iterate if you are way off the mark (more than three standard deviations). It is very important when setting objectives with customers to take into account any downstream **Service Level Objectives (SLO)** that you rely on.

> *"You're only as available as the sum of your dependencies."*
>
> *– The Calculus of Service Availability*

Your S3 bucket has an SLO of three nines (99.9%) and your EC2 instance's SLO is four nines (99.99%). The math gives you 99.98% for the combination. Add your software on top of that and your target value continues to decrease.

Agreements

Sit down with your customer and discuss your objectives. Discuss the cost of downtime. Identify where you have opportunities to improve and occasions to reduce your objectives. Time frames need to be addressed. Three nines over the course of a month (28 days) affords approximately 43 minutes of downtime. This is your error budget. Be clear with your users that it is within your right to have an inaccessible service for about 10 minutes every week if you agree on 99.9% as your point of agreement. On the other hand, you must consent to provide some level of renumeration when you exceed your error budget (start with something easy such as cookies). In the *Persistence Patterns* section, we will look at some strategies for leveraging data to build a continuous improvement process for your product.

Fault injection

In the meantime, start breaking things. Not in your user-facing environment. We have the ability to spin up copies of our service landscape using Terraform. By experimenting with failure in a low-risk place, it is possible to pinpoint potential deficiencies while minimizing blast radius. Netflix pioneered the emerging science of chaos engineering on AWS—more information can be found on the Chaos Monkey GitHub page (`https://netflix.github.io/chaosmonkey/`).

Reliability testing

In our earlier work with Terraform, we have seen how it requires a plan before an apply. This test-driven approach can be applied to our services too. Turn off an instance. No problem because our load balancer shifts all traffic to the other one. However, what happens if the load balancer disappears? Probably not good things. Luckily, AWS ALBs run across a number of instances. We shouldn't have a problem even though they have one. Is the inadvertent security rule change? That's probably going to cause a service interruption. Try it out in your sandbox by making the change in the AWS console. Get one of your colleagues to diagnose and troubleshoot it. Document how to resolve it. Automate the resolution. Keep learning.

Embrace risk

Creating a culture that is not afraid of failure is important. It might not be easy—lots of companies are afraid of risk and failure—but it is important; the math is not in your favor as system complexity grows. New features introduce risk; so does refactoring, as well as doing nothing. But for your product to grow, you must keep building features into it. The patterns we recommended during the previous chapter allow us to lessen our exposure to known hazards. Eliminating all danger is unrealistic.

Business continuity

We need to keep the product running even if human errors happen, or natural disasters or data corruption. In this section, we will look at ways Amazon helps us to lower our time to remedy some common disruptions. Good practices for incident management and post-mortems help us to stay within our error budgets while strengthening our services. In our metrics-driven engineering practice, we recommend exercising these processes regularly in order to fine tune your existing SLOs and identify any missing ones.

Snapshots

Just as we use S3 to replicate our objects, CodeCommit to protect our source, and ECR for the durability of our container images (in the next chapter), we can use disk snapshots to help us to safeguard our instance-attached storage:

```
resource "aws_ebs_volume" "example" {
  availability_zone = "us-west-2a"
  size = 40
  tags {
    Name = "HelloWorld"
  }
}

resource "aws_ebs_snapshot" "example_snapshot" {
  volume_id = "${aws_ebs_volume.example.id}"
  tags {
    Name = "HelloWorld_snap"
  }
}
```

Chapter 7

 For more details, check out https://www.terraform.io/docs/providers/aws/r/dlm_lifecycle_policy.html and https://docs.aws.amazon.com/AWSEC2/latest/UserGuide/snapshot-lifecycle.html.

The life cycle management (https://github.com/terraform-providers/terraform-provider-aws/pull/5558) of snapshots is still being worked on in Terraform. We will create a policy first:

```
resource "aws_iam_role" "snapshot_role" {
  name = "AWSDataLifecycleManagerDefaultRole"

  assume_role_policy = <<EOF
{
  "Version": "2012-10-17",
  "Statement": [
    {
      "Effect": "Allow",
      "Action": [
        "ec2:CreateSnapshot",
        "ec2:DeleteSnapshot",
        "ec2:DescribeVolumes",
        "ec2:DescribeSnapshots"
      ],
      "Resource": "*"
    },
    {
      "Effect": "Allow",
      "Action": [
        "ec2:CreateTags"
      ],
      "Resource": "arn:aws:ec2:*::snapshot/*"
    }
  ]
}
EOF
}
```

Now we can manage the life cycle through the CLI using this command:

```
aws dlm create-lifecycle-policy --description "ebs-snapshot-policy" --state ENABLED --execution-role-arn arn:aws:iam::12345678910:role/AWSDataLifecycleManagerDefaultRole --policy-details file://policyDetails.json
```

[129]

The policy file would look something like this:

```
{
  "ResourceTypes": [
    "VOLUME"
  ],
  "Schedules":[
    {
      "Name": "DailySnapshots",
      "TagsToAdd": [
        {
          "Key": "type",
          "Value": "myBookSnapshot"
        }
      ],
      "CreateRule": {
        "Interval": 24,
        "IntervalUnit": "HOURS",
        "Times": ["03:00"]
      },
      "RetainRule": {
        "Count":5
      }
    }
  ]
}
```

This life cycle policy will take a differential snapshot of our EBS disks every day at 3 A.M. and will keep five snapshots at all times.

Restore

At some point, we may need to recover the data from a snapshot. We need to explore whether a 24 hour loss of data is acceptable. This concept is called the **Recovery Point Objective (RPO)**. As with our service-level objectives, we need to understand our customer and business requirements to determine what the appropriate objective is. Now that we have come to an agreement with our stakeholders that a day is fine, we need to grasp the amount of data that we will need to restore. This will help to inform our **Recover Time Objective (RTO)**. Creating small volumes from a snapshot is a fast process. Detaching and re-attaching the volume to an instance can take a few minutes:

```
resource "aws_volume_attachment" "ebs_att" {
  device_name = "/dev/sdh"
  volume_id   = "${aws_ebs_volume.recoveryvolume.id}"
  instance_id = "${aws_instance.web.id}"
```

```
}
resource "aws_instance" "web" {
  ami = "ami-21f78e11"
  availability_zone = "us-west-2a"
  instance_type = "t1.micro"
  tags {
    Name = "cloudPatterns"
  }
}
resource "aws_ebs_volume" "recoveryvolume" {
  availability_zone = "us-west-2a"
  size = 1
  snapshot_id = "${aws_ebs_snapshot.example_snapshot.id}"
}
```

Practice this a few times to get the feel of what your objective should be. Another good recovery strategy involves using **Amazon Machine Images (AMI)** to improve your RTO. Create a new AMI from your latest snapshot and copy the AMI to other regions.

Disaster recovery

You should now be ready when calamities transpire. The Terraform scripts will be ready to go and your data just needs to be pointed at the new stuff or vice versa (we will touch on service discovery in the next chapter). Preparing ahead of time will aid you in handling demanding situations as they occur.

Incident response

We are not huge fans of writing documents that will be obsolete before the ink dries. However, in the case of an incident response plan, we'll make an exception. If you are running mission-critical services, the plan needs to take into account potential loss of life. For less crucial offerings, a simpler outline may suffice.

 We suggest you review Chapter 9 of the SRE Workbook (`https://www.oreilly.com/library/view/the-site-reliability/9781492029496/`) for a more in-depth look at incident management practices.

Postmortems

Getting stakeholders together after resolution of an incident is also imperative. Fast feedback on what went well, what kind of worked, and what failed during the downtime event and the process of handling it is crucial. A growth-oriented, learning organization encourages the evaluation to be blameless. It is very difficult to get honest criticism in a culture of fear. Building resilient systems at web scale is hard work.

Reduction

The goal of the practices in this chapter revolve around two distinct methods. The first is centered on reducing waste within operational practices. Defect reduction is the second tenet. Through automation and the reduction of manual work, you will have a healthier workplace. We have been focused on applying these principals to the cloud but they apply to your own workspace as well. The separation of code, configuration, and credentials ensures security at scale while allowing rapid prototyping, testing, and deployment.

Local development

While we have the luxury of Cloud9 in AWS, oftentimes you must do your initial unit testing locally. For this we recommend using tools such as Vagrant (https://www.vagrantup.com/), Packer (https://packer.io/), or Docker (https://www.docker.com/). In combination with Terraform, these tools allow you to start small and smoothly expand to Amazon. If you are already running virtualized workloads on premises, there are mechanisms to help you to migrate (https://aws.amazon.com/ec2/vm-import/) workloads to AWS. Another option is to extend (https://aws.amazon.com/vmware/) your existing data center onto AWS, augmenting your existing skills with the scalability of the cloud.

In the next section, we will explore non-compute-based options for moving services to Amazon. The breadth of data-driven options AWS furnishes will provide any organization with the opportunity to reduce their maintenance burden in order to focus on creating a competitive advantage for the product.

Summary

In this chapter, we covered how to break down silos within your organization. Practices for defining and measuring the success of your product among its users were introduced. Chaos testing and fault injection patterns were introduced as patterns that should be part of product operations. Taking advantage of systematic failures will allow you to identify opportunities to automate repetitive, non-value additive efforts. Combining these processes will help you to deliver a product with high availability and ensure that, in the case of a disaster, you have practiced your recovery methods.

Further reading

- Chapter 11 of *Lean Product Management* (https://www.packtpub.com/business/lean-product-management)
- Chapter 8 of *The Agile Developers Handbook* (https://www.packtpub.com/web-development/agile-developers-handbook)
- Chapter 4 of *Practical DevOps* (https://www.packtpub.com/virtualization-and-cloud/practical-devops-second-edition)
- Chapter 11 of *Practical Site Reliability Engineering* (https://www.packtpub.com/virtualization-and-cloud/practical-site-reliability-engineering)

8
Application Virtualization - Using Cloud Native Patterns for Your Workloads

Virtualization is not a new technology. However, the cloud has allowed us to abstract our programs further away from the underlying hardware. We began our journey creating AWS EC2 instances. The mechanism that the instance uses is the **virtual machine** (**VM**). Using a VM gives us the ability to share hardware at the operating system level. Windows, Linux, and iOS instances can all be run on VMs. Putting a hypervisor on top of the bare metal hardware gives Amazon the ability to run multiple OSes on a single piece of hardware or host. Packing many VMs onto a single host is a great way to increase utilization of expensive servers. Amazon's introduction of this model to the public created the modern-day cloud.

While AWS were selling, and securing, their spare capacity for multi-tenant use, the cloud model was extended into other areas. Networking was a big part of the second wave of virtualization. Isolation of workloads is critical in a shared services environment. As **Software-Defined Networking** (**SDN**) matured, the network boundary could also be moved away from physical **network interface controllers** (**NIC**).

In parallel to the development of hypervisors and SDN, a need to segregate processes running on an OS was also identified. A mechanism was needed beyond protecting the files and folders using **Access Control Lists** (**ACLs**). The feature that came about limits, accounts for, and isolates the resource usage (CPU, memory, disk I/O, network, and so on) of a collection of processes. Until recently, it required a deep understanding of the OS internals to manage the CGroup configurations. The Docker project coined the term **container** while simplifying the management required to insulate OS activities.

Amazon then went one step further with their **serverless** architecture. By providing a container with standardized dependencies built in, and a mechanism for further customization, the hurdles developers faced when delivering new features were lowered even further.

In this chapter, we will learn how to isolate services for performance improvements and cost savings. We will inspect choices available for reducing product complexity. Then we will review enterprise patterns for mitigating failures through the separation of concerns.

Technical requirements

We will be using Docker as our lightweight container management solution in this chapter. Instructions for installation are in the next section.

The code for this chapter can be found at `https://github.com/PacktPublishing/Implementing-Cloud-Design-Patterns-for-AWS-Second-Edition/tree/master/Chapter08`.

Please use the Cloud9 console to create a directory called `ch8` and change to it before you begin:

```
mkdir ch8 && cd ch8
```

Containers

Containerization is the method of packaging your applications for virtualization. The images created allow you to easily execute your containers in a variety of manners. We can install Docker on our Cloud9 instance:

```
sudo yum install -y docker
sudo service docker start
# The below command will tell us if the docker daemon is running
docker info
```

Let's look at a sample Dockerfile at `https://raw.githubusercontent.com/Docker-example/alpine-wordpress/master/Dockerfile`:

```
# Installing dependencies
RUN apk add --no-cache --virtual .build-deps unzip
RUN apk add --no-cache apache2 php7 php7-apache2 php7-openssl php7-xml php7-pdo php7-mcrypt php7-session php7-mysqli php7-zlib su-exec
RUN mkdir -p /run/apache2 /run/httpd
```

```
# Work path
WORKDIR /scripts
# Download & install wordpress
ADD https://wordpress.org/wordpress-${VERSION_WORDPRESS}.zip ./
RUN unzip -q wordpress-${VERSION_WORDPRESS}.zip -d ./ && \
    rm -rf ${APACHE_SERVER_PATH} && \
    mv wordpress/ ${APACHE_SERVER_PATH} && \
    rm /scripts/wordpress-${VERSION_WORDPRESS}.zip \
${APACHE_SERVER_PATH}/wp-config-sample.php \
        ${APACHE_SERVER_PATH}/license.txt \
${APACHE_SERVER_PATH}/readme.html && \
    chown -R apache:apache ${APACHE_SERVER_PATH} && \
    apk del .build-deps
# Copy of the HTTPD startup script
COPY ./scripts/start.sh ./start.sh
COPY ./files/wp-config.php ${APACHE_SERVER_PATH}/wp-config.php
EXPOSE 80
ENTRYPOINT [ "./start.sh" ]
```

Let's build the image:

`docker build -t sk-wordpress .`

The resultant image is compliant with the **Open Container Initiative** (**OCI**) image standard. It can be run by any container engine that is OCI compliant. We will run it with our local Docker daemon, but don't forget that the portability of this package is one of its biggest advantages (yay, cloud!):

`docker run -p 8081:80 hello-world`

In addition to a configuration file (https://github.com/Docker-example/alpine-wordpress/blob/master/files/wp-config.php) and a startup script (https://github.com/Docker-example/alpine-wordpress/blob/master/scripts/start.sh), that's all it takes to run WordPress as a container. We can use `curl` to validate that it's up:

`curl localhost:8081`

Containers gives us the ability to run our virtual applications on our own workstations with minimal effort. However, our image is only on our local machine. To make it in line with the practices we have been using throughout this book, we want to have them available in a version-controlled manner. Let's get the code into our CodeCommit repository first:

```
git add dockerfile
git commit -am 'wordpress dockerfile'
git push
```

Registry services

Now, we will use the AWS CLI to push our image out to the **Elastic Container Registry (ECR)**. This gives us the ability to share our image with our peers, or allow it to be accessed by automation in our build, test, and delivery steps:

```
resource "aws_ecr_repository" "ecs-cluster" {
  name = " sk-wordpress"
}
```

Get your account ID from the TF output:

```
docker tag hello-world <aws_account_id>.dkr.ecr.us-east-1.amazonaws.com/sk-wordpress
aws ecr get-login --no-include-email
docker push aws_account_id.dkr.ecr.us-east-1.amazonaws.com/hello-world
```

ECR is also based on community standards. Migrating the bundle to another provider is just as simple. Migrating into an S3 bucket can be done using a few commands.

Elastic Container Service

Amazon's container service is a great option for building distributed clusters in a geographically distributed fashion. There is a good deal of complexity in managing it yourself. In the name of toil reduction, we will skip that part and take advantage of the newer Fargate offering to deliver our containers in an easier manner:

```
resource "aws_ecs_cluster" "ecs-cluster" {
  name = "sk-cluster"
}

resource "aws_ecs_service" "sk-wordpress" {
  name = "wordpress"
  cluster = "${aws_ecs_cluster.ecs-cluster.id}"
  launch_type = "FARGATE "
  task_definition = "${aws_ecs_task_definition.wordpress.arn}"
  desired_count = 2
  iam_role = "${aws_iam_role.ecs-cluster.arn}"
  depends_on = ["aws_iam_role_policy.ecs-cluster"]
  network_configuration {
    security_groups = ["${var.security_groups_ids}", "${aws_security_group.ecs_service.id}"]
    subnets = ["${var.subnets_ids}"]
  }
  load_balancer {
```

```
    target_group_arn = "${aws_lb_target_group.ecs-cluster.arn}"
    container_name   = "wordpress"
    container_port   = 8080
  }
}
```

Managed Kubernetes service

Amazon has also recently introduced a Kubernetes service called EKS. Google made the Kubernetes code open source after many years of using it to run containerized workloads in their private data centers. Kubernetes lets you easily migrate workloads across infrastructure providers and internal or public clouds. It is gaining considerable traction among vendors who want to easily deliver a microservice-oriented product regardless of the cloud. Some of the functionality Kubernetes provides duplicates the ones AWS offers. In most cases, these are all software-based. The trade-offs for using the native Kubernetes offerings are too large to cover in this book. Even though Kubernetes was released in 2014, the ecosystem growing around it is still developing. Rapid changes are occurring as it's introduced to environments outside of Google. YAML is used for Kubernetes configuration and there is a popular package manager called Helm. Most of the steps to install Kubernetes using Terraform have already been covered in this book.

Serverless

Functions as a service allow us to decouple development and deployment efforts more easily using containers or Kubernetes. However, there are additional complexities that arise when using a serverless architecture. Amazon simplifies the security, storage, and aggression components with their other servers very well.

Let's take a look at how we can set up a Lambda tied to a CloudFront distribution that points to our WordPress container. We will build a Lambda function that inspects the header of the request and sends it depending upon the information contained in that header.

First let's create our CloudFront Lambda file as `cloudfront_lambda.js`:

```
'use strict';

exports.handler = (event, context, callback) => {
    const request = event.Records[0].cf.request;
    const headers = request.headers;
```

```javascript
    if (request.uri !== '/index.html') {
        // do not process if this is not an A-B test request
        callback(null, request);
        return;
    }

    const cookieExperimentA = 'X-Experiment-Name=A';
    const cookieExperimentB = 'X-Experiment-Name=B';
    const pathExperimentA = '/index.html';
    const pathExperimentB = '/indexB.html';

    let experimentUri;
    if (headers.cookie) {
        for (let i = 0; i < headers.cookie.length; i++) {
            if (headers.cookie[i].value.indexOf(cookieExperimentA) >= 0) {
                console.log('Experiment A cookie found');
                experimentUri = pathExperimentA;
                break;
            } else if (headers.cookie[i].value.indexOf(cookieExperimentB) >= 0) {
                console.log('Experiment B cookie found');
                experimentUri = pathExperimentB;
                break;
            }
        }
    }

    if (!experimentUri) {
        console.log('Experiment cookie has not been found. Throwing dice...');
        if (Math.random() < 0.75) {
            experimentUri = pathExperimentA;
        } else {
            experimentUri = pathExperimentB;
        }
    }

    request.uri = experimentUri;
    console.log(`Request uri set to "${request.uri}"`);
    callback(null, request);
};
```

This is a adapted from https://docs.aws.amazon.com/AmazonCloudFront/latest/DeveloperGuide/lambda-examples.html.

Let's compress it for upload to the S3 bucket:

```
zip cloudfront_lambda.zip cloudfront_lambda.js
```

Now, we can create the lambda in Terraform. Let's call it `cloudfront_lambda_terraform.tf`:

```
resource "aws_iam_role" "iam_for_lambda" {
  name = "iam_for_lambda"

  assume_role_policy = <<EOF
{
  "Version": "2012-10-17",
  "Statement": [
    {
      "Action": "sts:AssumeRole",
      "Principal": {
        "Service": "lambda.amazonaws.com"
      },
      "Effect": "Allow"
    },
    {
      "Action": "sts:AssumeRole",
      "Principal": {
        "Service": "edgelambda.amazonaws.com"
      },
      "Effect": "Allow"
    },
  ]
}
EOF
}

resource "aws_lambda_function" "cloudfront_terraform_lambda" {
  filename = "cloudfront_lambda.zip"
  function_name = "cloudfront_terraform_lambda"
  role = "${aws_iam_role.iam_for_lambda.arn}"
  handler = "cloudfront_lambda.handler"
  runtime = "nodejs8.10"
  source_code_hash = "${base64sha256(file("cloudfront_lambda.zip"))}"
  publish = "true"
}
```

Next, we will create a CloudFront distribution using Terraform and associate it with our lambda. We will call it `cloudfront_lambda.tf`:

```
resource "aws_s3_bucket" "cloudpatterns-cloudfrontbucket" {
  bucket = "cloudpatterns-cloudfront"
  acl = "public-read"
  website {
    index_document = "index.html"
  }

  tags = {
    Name = "My cloudfront bucket"
  }
}
```

```
resource "aws_cloudfront_distribution" "s3_distribution" {
  origin {
    domain_name = "${aws_s3_bucket.cloudpatterns-cloudfrontbucket.bucket_domain_name}"
    origin_id = "cloudpatterns-cloudfront"
  }

  enabled = true
  default_root_object = "index.html"

  default_cache_behavior {
    allowed_methods = ["DELETE", "GET", "HEAD", "OPTIONS", "PATCH", "POST", "PUT"]
    cached_methods = ["GET", "HEAD"]
    target_origin_id = "cloudpatterns-cloudfront"
    lambda_function_association {
      event_type = "viewer-request"
      lambda_arn = "${aws_lambda_function.cloudfront_terraform_lambda.qualified_arn}"
      include_body = false
    }
```

```
  restrictions {
    geo_restriction {
      restriction_type = "none"
    }
  }

  tags = {
    Environment = "production"
  }
```

Chapter 8

```
    viewer_certificate {
      cloudfront_default_certificate = true
    }
}
```

Let's run our Terraform:

`terraform init && terraform apply`

You will see a CloudFront domain in the Terraform output. It will look something like this.

```
aws_cloudfront_distribution.s3_distribution: Creation complete after 1s
(ID: EWZL7KYFCHTVR)
```

Take a look at your AWS console to find the DNS name:

We did not attach this CloudFront distribution to our container or domain. Testing will be done with the `curl` command for simplicity.

> A CloudFront distribution takes a while to complete.

Run the following two commands with your distribution name and you will see the two different index pages that we created in the bucket previously:

```
curl --header "Cookie: X-Experiment-Name=A"
http://d30mh0bj27uhwf.cloudfront.net/index.html
 curl --header "Cookie: X-Experiment-Name=B"
http://d30mh0bj27uhwf.cloudfront.net/index.html
```

[143]

Application Virtualization – Using Cloud Native Patterns for Your Workloads

The following screenshot displays the output of the preceding commands:

```
cloudpatterns:~/environment/cloudpatternsrepo/Chapter5 (master) $ curl --header "Cookie: X-Experiment-Name=A" http://d30mh0bj27uhwf.cloudfront.net/index.html
Hello world from Terraform!cloudpatterns:~/environment/cloudpatternsrepo/Chapter5 (master) $ curl --header "Cookie: X-Experiment-Name=B" http://d30mh0bj27uhwf.cloudfront.net/index.html
Hello world from TerraformB!cloudpatterns:~/environment/cloudpatternsrepo/Chapter5 (master) $
```

In this case, we are using CloudFront's default caching mechanisms. We will look into other, more robust caching alternatives in Chapter 10, *Databases – Identifying which Type Fits Your Needs*.

 The Edge Lambda is considerably more expensive than the standard Lambda function, so in cases where you want to significantly increase response time or decrease latency, it is an excellent choice. However, where those concerns are not as important, it is better to attach your Lambda to a load balancer instead of the CloudFront distribution.

In this example, we will configure our load balancer to use a Lambda function, which will direct traffic to our S3 bucket/WordPress container in most cases. When we have an outage or the service is not available, it will failover to the static S3 bucket instead. This acts as a rudimentary circuit breaker for our application. The benefits of this graceful degradation will be covered in the next chapter.

First, we will create a Lambda function as `alb_lambda.js`:

```javascript
'use strict';

exports.handler = (event, context, callback) => {
    const request = event;
    const headers = request.headers;
    const host = headers.host;

    if (request.path !== '/') {
        // do not process if this is not an A-B test request
        callback(null, response);
        return;
    }

    const cookieExperimentA = 'X-Experiment-Name=A';
    const cookieExperimentB = 'X-Experiment-Name=B';
    const pathExperimentA = '/index.html';
    const pathExperimentB = '/indexB.html';

    let experimentUri;
    if (headers.cookie === cookieExperimentB ) {
        console.log('Experiment B cookie found');
        experimentUri = pathExperimentB;
    } else {
```

```
            console.log('No valid cookie found');
            experimentUri = pathExperimentA;
    }

    if (!experimentUri) {
        console.log('Experiment cookie has not been found. Throwing
dice...');
        if (Math.random() < 0.75) {
            experimentUri = pathExperimentA;
        } else {
            experimentUri = pathExperimentB;
        }
    }

    request.uri = experimentUri;
    const anArray = ["statusCode", "body", "headers"];
    const locationObject = "http://${host}${request.uri}"
    const anObject = { statusCode: "301", body: null, headers:
"${locationObject}" };
    const response = JSON.stringify({
      anObject,
      anArray,
      another: "item"
    });
    console.log(`Request uri set to "http://${host}${request.uri}"`);
    callback(null, response);
};
```

Zip it up for deployment:

```
zip alb_lambda.zip alb_lambda.js
```

Next, we will create an ALB and attach the Lambda as a target group in alb.tf:

```
resource "aws_lb" "lambda-alb" {
  name = "lambda-lb-tf"
  internal = false
  load_balancer_type = "application"
  subnets = ["subnet-447dd623","subnet-476f170d"]
}

resource "aws_lb_listener" "alb_listener" {
  load_balancer_arn = "${aws_lb.lambda-alb.arn}"
  port = "80"
  protocol = "HTTP"
  default_action {
    target_group_arn = "${aws_lb_target_group.lambda-target-group.arn}"
    type = "forward"
```

```
  }
}

resource "aws_lb_target_group" "lambda-target-group" {
  name = "alb-lambda-group"
  target_type = "lambda"
}

resource "aws_lb_target_group_attachment" "lamdba-target-attachment" {
  target_group_arn = "${aws_lb_target_group.lambda-target-group.arn}"
  target_id = "${aws_lambda_function.alb_terraform_lambda.arn}"
  depends_on = ["aws_lambda_permission.iam_for_alb"]
}
```

 ALBs require two subnets. I just picked them from my default VPC. They need to be in different availability zones.

We will create our new Lambda and ensure that our load balancer is the only object with the permission to execute the function by adding the following to `cloudfront_lambda_terraform.tf`:

```
resource "aws_lambda_permission" "iam_for_alb" {
  statement_id = "AllowExecutionFromlb"
  action = "lambda:InvokeFunction"
  function_name = "alb_lambda"
  principal = "elasticloadbalancing.amazonaws.com"
  source_arn = "${aws_lb_target_group.lambda-target-group.arn}"
}

resource "aws_lambda_function" "alb_terraform_lambda" {
  filename = "alb_lambda.zip"
  function_name = "alb_lambda"
  role = "${aws_iam_role.iam_for_lambda.arn}"
  handler = "alb_lambda.handler"
  runtime = "nodejs8.10"
  source_code_hash = "${base64sha256(file("alb_lambda.zip"))}"
  publish = "true"
}
```

Run the following two commands with your load balancer name and you will see the two different index pages we created in the preceding bucket:

```
curl --header "Cookie: X-Experiment-Name=A"
http://lambda-lb-tf-1962503085.us-east-1.elb.amazonaws.com
curl --header "Cookie: X-Experiment-Name=B"
http://lambda-lb-tf-1962503085.us-east-1.elb.amazonaws.com
```

Serverless is a great paradigm for advanced organizations. When you begin to add multiple services, it gets harder to keep track of things. In the next section, we will look at some additional alternatives for simplifying the location of ever-changing endpoints.

Service discovery

We have already explored one method that can assist with service discovery: the load balancer. Amazon provides three different types of load balancers, any of which could potentially front your service in a region. In Chapter 2, *Core Services - Building Blocks for Your Product*, we looked at load balancer health checks for monitoring your instances. In the *Serverless* section, we explored fronting our Lambda services with a load balancer. We could have added a health check for the serverless implementation as well. Creating a target group for ECS containers is another pattern available to us. Using a load balancer provides highly available internal or external service endpoints. There are also a number of other options we can use in conjunction with ELBs and ALBs.

Route 53 provides us with the ability to create global load balancers. In contrast to the ALB, which provides load balancing at the port level, Route 53 distributes traffic across hostnames using DNS. It is quite easy to add multiple regional ALBs to a DNS record. There are similar options for health checks and failover, which should be put in place as well. Service routing can be altered by changing from the default `round-robin` policy. Instead of using the first record, then the next, it is possible to weight DNS records. Heavier routes will be sent more traffic. By changing weights, you can effect a canary style rollout of new service versions across regions. Latency-based weighting looks at historical data captured by Amazon and sends requests along the least congested paths. If speedy responses are your priority, use this option.

Finally, if you are using Docker for your containers, the links mechanism provides a simple method for connecting your services. The AWS Service Discovery Service collects your container services endpoints and adds them to a cloud map, providing a global view of your catalog. EKS also provides operators that allow you to use Route 53 as a dynamic service registry. For developer use, you should also review the use of **namespaces** for Kubernetes. We would hazard that AWS will offer a similar service-discovery mechanism for Kubernetes shortly. One of the key benefits of native links and namespaces is that you can reuse the same tags locally for development as you do for production in AWS. This decreases the configuration burden, streamlines integration testing, and simplifies service deployment.

Summary

In this chapter, we learned how Amazon's abstraction has evolved from virtual machines to individual functions. After checking out how we can package and deliver a containerized application, we looked at how the serverless model allows us to bundle our code with even fewer dependencies. Isolation of the smallest parts of your product can ease development and deployment efforts.

In the next chapter, we will attend to the difficulties we might encounter as our product complexity grows.

Further reading

- For more information on Lambda, check out: https://aws.amazon.com/lambda/serverless-architectures-learn-more/
- Complex cloud virtualization strategies can be found in the *VMware Cross-Cloud Architecture* book: https://www.packtpub.com/virtualization-and-cloud/vmware-cross-cloud-architecture
- A video introduction to Kubernetes is available at https://www.packtpub.com/application-development/kubernetes-absolute-beginners-hands-video and advanced patterns and practices are covered in this book: https://www.packtpub.com/virtualization-and-cloud/kubernetes-design-patterns-and-extensions

9
Antipatterns - Avoiding Counterproductive Solutions

We have looked at a number of good processes, practices, and patterns for the AWS cloud. Now, we will explore some that you want to avoid. Some of the examples that follow are going to be countered by using the items in the first two sections. Others are not inherently technology problems. You should be aware of the smells that they bring and change course when you run into them. As your cloud craftsmanship improves, they will be easier to spot before implementation. At the beginning of your cloud journey, we expect failure to occur all the time. Be aware that refactoring is always going to be an option moving past your minimum viable product. Often, speed is the most important dimension to your product success. Taking on technical debt may be required to increase market shares or drive new features.

We will briefly cover the following topics in this chapter:

- Exploring counterproductive processes
- Practices to avoid in general
- Anti-patterns that you might come across

Exploring counterproductive processes

The first category we will explore is counterproductive processes. The cloud provides a whole new set of features that you can take advantage of. Migrating existing processes to your AWS-based product will work in most cases, but you will miss out on a great opportunity to make things better. Doing things the same way in the cloud will lead you back to where you are today. Consider how you add the greatest value for your customer before you spend time repeating what you did before the cloud existed.

The sections that follow cover processes that can be used, but probably shouldn't.

Lift and shift

Wholesale migration of your existing systems, products, practices, and patterns to AWS is our first anti-pattern. You can do it, but seriously think about it. If your only objective is cost savings and you have no plans to ever change your product offerings, go for it. However, you will end up loading even more technical debt onto your teams. This will make it even harder to change course when the market eventually shifts away from what you are doing. Small experiments with cloud migration will be a better solution while lessening your systemic risk.

Change control boards

If you have a complicated change review process, it's recommended that you reduce or remove this process before you move to AWS. Following test-driven, peer reviewed development practices for your product provides additional benefits without all the bureaucracy typically found in a **change control board** (CCB). In conjunction with desilofication (covered later in this chapter), the removal of this step will increase your time-to-value immensely.

That's not to say that removing the CCB is going to be an easy task. CCB's are usually in place to provide companies with a feeling of security and the ability to manage risk – sometimes, deployments are seen as just plain risky.

Non-reproducibility

Manual processes are inherently risky. We have all typed in the wrong password or forgotten to close a quote. Let your automation take care of as much as possible. If you find yourself doing the same thing more than twice, seriously consider automating it. The whole industry is moving in the direction of idempotence (the property of certain operations that allows users to repeatedly make the same call without producing any change to the initial result). The microservice and serverless patterns give us the ability to minimize variation within our systems.

Firefighting

Remember all that technical debt you created by ignoring the previous three smells? At some point, things will start exploding (if they're not burning already). If you find yourself trying to contain a tire fire, your product will suffer the most. All the time you could have dedicated to delighting your users will be wasted dousing flare-ups. The next section will cover some of the data we can use to speed up the smothering. Breathing in some smoke occasionally is fine. Not ever seeing which direction you are going will asphyxiate your product.

Can't fail attitude to system uptime

Being in a place where your product cannot fail is good if lives depend on your system. Any place else, you need to expect breakdowns. If you are not running a mission-critical system and people are telling you that failure is not an option, it might be time to find another job. The number of combinations you can put together with AWS services, coupled with duplication to ensure availability, integrity, and confidentiality increases the odds of a deficiency. Chaotic engineering experiments can build confidence in a system. Concise service level agreements help build consumer confidence and manage customer expectations about possible downtime.

Practices to avoid in general

There is going to be some overlap here with the previous section, but we will focus on behaviors at a higher level. As you move to the AWS cloud, you have an excuse to review your traditional methods to ensure they are still applicable. In most cases, the technology is not the largest inhibiting factor. A lack of shared understanding will be the biggest blocker.

The following sections cover some of the most common practices that should be avoided.

Silos

Conway's law (http://www.melconway.com/Home/Conways_Law.html) suggests that an organization is bound to create software that mimics its structure. Think about this as you move your workloads to the cloud. There is an opportunity to refactor your team, as well as your systems and software. Organizational design is out of the scope of this book, but we will touch on some patterns to aid you in implementing good development practices later in the chapter.

The outcome of those exercises will provide input to the desilofication that should be done before you get too far in your cloud journey. An easy win in this analysis is usually to be found in your testing and quality assurance areas. As we discussed earlier, moving these processes forward in your development process will bear rewards in the velocity and quality spaces. Involving your security teams straightaway will also lessen your process waste.

Lock in

Organizational composition can also force you into sub-optimal patterns. Discussions with the same old people can get you stuck in a rut that it is difficult to clamber out of. Out-of-the-box thinking needs to be encouraged, as there is no box except the one you put yourself into. On a similar note, try to avoid solutions with a single option. Try to choose technologies that adhere to well-known standards and offer a pool of competing alternatives.

Amazon offers a great many operating systems from which to choose for your instances. EKS is built on Kubernetes, which is a mature project maintained by a well-established foundation (`https://www.cncf.io/projects/`). Open source roots also give you the ability to contribute back to the community and protect yourself from forced retirement of a component.

Version control

Keeping track of components such as code, configurations, and credentials is crucial. There are many people who will tell you that everyone should commit to master, while others espouse the benefits of branches. We will not get into that. If you do not keep old revisions of everything, it will catch up with you. Components must be handled in a way that allows for retrieval of previous iterations. The ability to mix new options of one with the other during testing is crucial to continual experimentation and long-term cloud success.

Anti-patterns that you might come across

AWS is awesome. Companies like Hacker News, Reddit, and Instagram could never have succeeded without its utility form. The challenge is not to recreate your current problems in the cloud. For startups who are building from scratch, it is easy to fall into the same traps that have historically slowed innovation and diminished security. The evolution of microservices occurred because dependency management and release coordination are difficult problems to solve over the course of a lifetime for a large product.

The following sections cover some anti-patterns, usually used in traditional deployment environments, that can be translated into AWS environments.

Monoliths

You certainly can paint yourself into a corner with AWS. In order to speed your product to market, you will build a **big ball of mud** (https://en.wikipedia.org/wiki/Big_ball_of_mud). Even large companies can find themselves in a mess with many services being created, but with little forward-planning. As a counter to this, organizations like Amazon and Netflix use **microservices** – small services tailored to do only one thing, but to do it well.

The Rise of Microservices website (https://www.appcentrica.com/the-rise-of-microservices/) details more about how microservices came about, how and why they are used, and how to handle them in production.

At some point, you will be able to take a breath and address all the technical debt you have accumulated, or everything will blow up at a very inconvenient time. Recognizing when to refactor is key. Using explicit techniques such as bounded context from the **Domain-Driven Design** world (https://vaughnvernon.co/) will help you decompose your monolith into microservices. Be advised though: as with everything there are trade-offs. Managing several microservices, let alone many hundreds or even thousands of microservices, is, in itself, a complicated task.

Single points of failure

Netflix has run into all kinds of issues on AWS. Estimates suggest that one-quarter of the traffic on the internet is theirs. Amazon is always improving their products in order to delight their customers, but also to eliminate single points of failure. Global customers provide the insight to build more reliable services while maintaining availability and low cost. Common occurrences of **single points of failure** in non-cloud environments were usually found in the connectivity realm – or rather, networking (see the following subsection). Other elements that can be seen as single points of failure are data stores and web-service hosting environments/application servers, where only single instances are used. Having environments without redundancy is usually a sign of bad design.

Networking

One key benefit of the Amazon Cloud is its abundance of addresses. In the past, the **Internet Protocol** (**IP**) version 4 furnished us with a large address space. Now that there are billions of mobile phones on the planet, we are running out of headroom. **Network Address Translation** (**NAT**) supplied us with a workaround to the challenge. Although NAT will keep us going for years to come, IPv6 is the future. Each person on the planet can be assigned trillions of addresses at a time without exhausting the pool. Consider using IPv6 for your internal networks moving forward to eliminate complex NATing schemes. The flexibility to change easily outweighs the burden of NAT. If you must use NAT, ensure that your DNS, load balancers, and instances can be quickly recreated in a new region (the low-cost option). For critical components, ensure availability through fault-tolerant designs. Don't forget about your gateways, networks, and routes.

Scaling

Netflix ran into more classes of failures as they scaled. They propagated feedback loops that took their own systems offline. These downstream effects were mitigated by some new patterns lifted from traditional engineering disciplines. First, they began using caches to reduce to load on postliminary systems. Eventually, up-to-date systems were good enough for many of their products. Next, came bulkheads. This construct allows developers to mirror the divide provided by availability zones and regions in their software.

Chapter 9

Resilience

The following screenshot shows the Hystrix (https://github.com/Netflix/Hystrix) dashboard for a Spring Boot (http://spring.io/projects/spring-boot) application. The circuit breaker was one of the first patterns Netflix put into place to help product owners provide graceful degradation in a consistent manner:

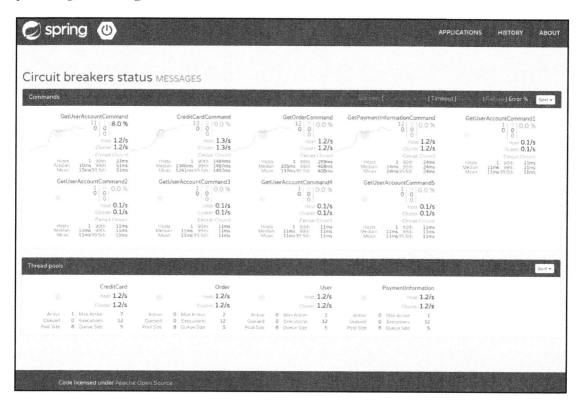

The preceding screenshot can be found at https://github.com/VanRoy/spring-cloud-dashboard/blob/master/screenshot-circuit-breaker.png.

When building resilient systems, timeouts are notoriously difficult to manage. Both upstream and downstream dependencies can provide their own settings, and managing the aggregates can be a delicate operation. By allowing for a valid response code in the event of insufficient capacity, Netflix products exhibited graceful degradation in the event of any timeout. Amazon adopted many of these models for their own retail properties. Rate limiting, bulkheading, automatic retries, and response caching patterns equip your product developers with tried and true methods to respond to cloud-scale traffic bursts.

Summary

We have looked at solutions that are ineffective and may result in undesired consequences. Avoiding these cloud anti-patterns promotes increased quality and lower defects throughout your cloud adventure. We have covered how to eschew recreating organization barriers in AWS, recognize unsuitable cloud workloads, and regularly detect opportunities for improvement. In the next chapter, we will identify how to collect and learn from data that can help us avoid anomalies that haven't been widely encountered in the cloud yet.

Further reading

- *AWS Networking Essential* (`https://subscription.packtpub.com/video/virtualization_and_cloud/9781788299190`).
- Refer to `Chapter 1`, *Breaking the Monolith* for bounded context, and `Chapter 4`, *Client Patterns* and `Chapter 5`, *Reliability Patterns* for patterns of the *Microservices Development Cookbook* (`https://subscription.packtpub.com/book/application_development/9781788479509`) book.
- *DevOps with Git* (`https://subscription.packtpub.com/video/application_development/9781789618839`).
- *resilience4j* (`https://github.com/resilience4j/resilience4j`) delivers Java exemplars you can reuse in your code.
- Envoy (`https://www.envoyproxy.io/`) is a container-based solution that can centralize many of the configuration responsibilities of developers.

Section 3: Persistence Patterns

In this section, you will learn how to recognize approaches to common persistence problems that have been formalized and that are generally considered good development practice.

The following chapters are included in this section:

- `Chapter 10`, *Databases – Identifying Which Type Fits Your Needs*
- `Chapter 11`, *Data Processing – Handling Your Data Transformation*
- `Chapter 12`, *Observability – Understanding How Your Products Are Behaving*
- `Chapter 13`, *Anti-Patterns – Bypassing Inferior Options*

10
Databases - Identifying Which Type Fits Your Needs

Successful cloud products rely on a combination of patterns for static data, such as cache distribution, direct hosting, and web storage hosting. We will investigate patterns for data replication, in-memory caching, and sharding throughout this chapter. Persistence methods will also be reviewed for applicability to cloud native applications. This will help you to design your cloud infrastructure persistence layers. In this chapter, you will be able to select the right data service for the product as well as understand how to serve static content. Also, you'll see how indexing your data contributes to fast retrieval and gain an understanding of aggregating your data for compression purposes.

The following topics will be covered in this chapter in brief:

- General considerations:
    - Vertical versus horizontal scaling
    - Rate of change—static versus dynamic
- Relational data services:
    - Transactional data
    - CAP Theorem
    - Aurora and MySQL
- Polyglot persistence:
    - ElasticSearch
    - CloudTrail
    - Elemental MediaStore
    - **Elastic MapReduce (EMR)**
    - Neptune
    - Timestream

General considerations

In this section, we will discuss the general considerations that you need to have when designing your application infrastructure. Whilst some of these decisions will only be fleshed out by performing experiments and gaining experience with the tools, many of the solutions that AWS provide are industry standard and are generally well known.

We will cover the following:

- Considerations around workflow
- Determining which type of scaling is appropriate for different situations
- How to plan for durability and ensure reliability and data access speed
- Ensuring that you're sizing your storage sufficiently

We'll finish our discussion by covering different types of data and storage engines that we have available to us. This will not be exhaustive coverage of everything that AWS provides: that would create a manual several orders of magnitude than we have space for.

Workflow

In the beginning, workflows were relatively simple. You wrote all of your database changes locally as SQL scripts, tested those against your local instance, then had them rolled out to your production server either by yourself, or, if you were lucky enough to have one, a DBA. Database change scripts, once the changes had been made, were generally discarded—no record of the change or why it was necessary was kept, at least not by the development team.

With the introduction of concepts such as object relational modeling and frameworks that manage their own database changes, the older practices have started to die out. Using a framework's migration facility—in this case, migration refers to the (usually) reversible set of database changes managed by a framework—has one major additional benefit: you have a history of database changes committed into your source repository, placed under the same scrutiny and protections as other code changes.

As the database changes travel with the code through the build chain, automated build tools can run these changes as part of the build process, again using the same scrutiny and toolsets used for code testing and quality analysis.

This means that the changes are run in a reliable way and, in this manner, propagate to any environments that you might be using in your test/acceptance chain and your production environment.

Data migration into AWS is made easier by using the data migration service, although you are free to migrate your data manually should you so wish.

Vertical versus horizontal scaling

In most cases, when first starting out with AWS, the entire application stack (this is sometimes called a **monolith**) would be deployed to a single instance that initially would have sufficient capacity (CPU and RAM) to handle the expected load. When we start adding additional resources, to increase the amount of RAM or available CPU of that instance, we are said to be scaling vertically. Sometimes, this is sufficient for our needs. Sometimes, it isn't. Vertical scaling will only get you so far, as it becomes more expensive to host your application on a single instance, rather than use multiple smaller instances and spread the load. The following diagram depicts scaling deployment infrastructure vertically:

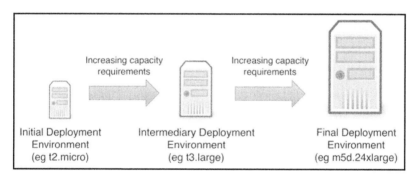

Part of software design is to understand this. To address this issue, it becomes necessary to break the application into separate dedicated tiers that decouple parts of the application; this could be moving toward an n-tier application or maybe even micro-services. The drive is to start extracting the application state so that it is essentially separate from the application. The aim is to make the application more or less stateless. When this is achieved, the application can be split out across more than one machine/instance.

Once we start doing this, we've started scaling the infrastructure horizontally, which is depicted in the following diagram:

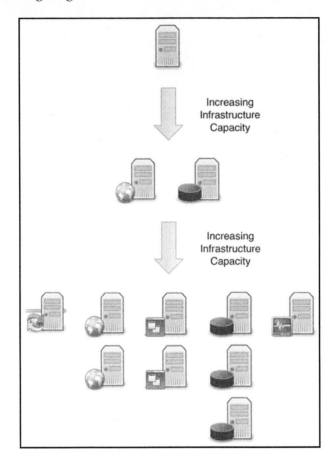

Horizontal scaling is achieved with the assistance of load balancing (ELB), distributed filesystems, and clustering. These help to maintain consistency of the response and availability of services. Much of contemporary software design—paradigms such as service-oriented architecture and microservices—favors many small systems working together: small instances sharing load, which in turn increases the fault-tolerance, reliability, and stability of the system and reduces cost.

How does this relate to managing a database on AWS? In the initial stages—when only running on, say, one small general ECS instance backed by an EBS volume—vertical scaling would mean that you need to provision more capacity for the EBS volume (up to 16 TB at present). Horizontal scaling means that you would need to load balance across a number of such ECS instances (each with its own EBS volume or use), or scale across a number of storage-optimized ECS instances (that have internal storage options—ideal, incidentally, for databases).

Durability—surviving system failure

It is inevitable that your system will fail from time to time. Regardless of how robust you think your infrastructure is, something will happen that will cause catastrophic failure and it could range from preventable null pointer exceptions through to *act of God* events such as lightning strikes, floods, and earthquakes.

If you've designed your system to use AWS managed services, such as **Relational Data Services** (**RDS**)—for instance, DynamoDB or ElasticSearch services, among others—you will mostly likely benefit from the high availability, auto-updating, auto-backup, and multi-regional redundancy that these services can provide.

If you don't use managed services, you need to take redundancy, availability, updates, and backup/recovery into account. The system that holds your application needs to be designed so that partial failure of nodes can be handled, but also so that, should catastrophic failure happen, it can be recovered in short order. This means that you'll need to design a backup and recovery process that suits your organization.

Dimensions

If you are manually provisioning your databases, you will need to determine adequate space for all of your data needs and possibly determine some *growing room:* additional provisioned space that you can grow into before you need to think about how you want to scale your application. Refer back to the section on *Vertical versus horizontal scaling* earlier in this chapter for a reminder if you need it.

Should you not wish to have concerns around scaling your data storage needs, then a managed service is the way to go. AWS managed services auto-scale (or auto-provision, depending on which service it is).

Reliability

It is obviously important that access to your database is reliable. Reliability can be achieved in many different ways. Having a single database instance is never ideal—it forms a single point of failure, so if your database disappears, it takes everything built on top of it down as well.

Different types of database handle reliability in different ways. Traditionally, RDBMS have been used in write master and read slave configurations: data is written to one (or more) *masters* and then the data is distributed through an internal replication mechanism to the rest of the system once it has been confirmed.

Latterly, and more prevalently in NoSQL datastores, the data is distributed across a number of shards, maintained internally by the datastore itself. As the data is sharded across a number of nodes, rather than replicated, there is a chance that, when a node is lost, some data could be lost too, at least until it can be restored from other shards or from backup storage.

Load balancers can also be used to manage data flow between database nodes and the application servers in your infrastructure.

Read versus write

In most cases, it is far quicker to access and read data from a database than it is to write to one. Many database systems, both NoSQL and RDBMS, tend to lock tables/collections for writing, making write a serial operation: multiple writes to the same table happen one after another, whereas reading data from (unlocked) tables is generally a parallel operation, and multiple reads happen at the same time. The reasons for this difference are legion, but they mostly boil down to this: writing data is a mutating process, whereas reading is not.

Something else to consider is that writing to a database is also a relatively time-consuming operation. At a very high level, writing involves the following steps:

1. Establish a connection.
2. Find the table.
3. Lock the table.
4. Write data.
5. Check consistency/conformity.

6. Perform any necessary index operations.
7. Unlock the table.
8. Close the connection.

Reading data is usually much simpler (again, at a very high level), as is shown here:

1. Establish a connection.
2. Scan the indexes.
3. Retrieve the data.
4. Close the connection.

Latency

A big factor in the use of databases is the amount of time it takes to access the data, be that read or write. This is called latency and has a large impact on the responsiveness of your application. The more frequently you need to access the datastore, the slower things can get.

There are some things that can be done to reduce the latency of accessing the datastore: batching queries from the application, indexing frequently accessed data, and increasing the amount of available memory or CPU all help.

For NoSQL types, such as MongoDB, having frequently accessed data held in memory is best—this requires a large amount of RAM, though. For relational or transactional databases, it's sometimes better to cache frequently accessed data in a separate key-value store such as Redis. Having separate read and write instances and using data replication between the two is also an industry standard solution. Obviously, there are further considerations with caching, such as staleness of data, but these are usually not difficult problems to solve.

Lastly, something to consider is that some data services provided by AWS are *eventually consistent*, which is particularly the case for DynamoDB and S3 Buckets. This means that data written to the service will take some amount of time to be distributed to all of the read nodes of the store (for DynamoDB, this is typically less than 1s for all nodes to converge), so it won't be instantly available. What this might mean in reality is that a query might return stale data if you perform a read query against data written less than a second or so ago. This may or may not be acceptable, depending on your use case.

Rate of change—static versus dynamic

Some data used by your application/system will always need to be kept current: this means persistent access to read, write, and update. That's the whole point of having the datastore in the first place. Elements within this data, though, will need updating much less frequently—configuration data or language translations, for example, are frequently written to the database just once and then read as required. They are rarely, if ever, updated. At the other end of the scale, product pricing or sports data might need to be updated several times a day, or even more frequently. Greyhound race data, for example, needs updating several times a second during an event, but then becomes static thereafter.

Understanding the life cycle of the data that is used by your product is key. That will influence the type of datastore that you require.

Some of this data is cacheable; some isn't. Part of the design of your application and the infrastructure around it is to determine which data is predominately static and which is transactional, and assign each to a datastore that is appropriate for that use case.

For static assets, serving directly from S3 buckets is an option.

Access frequency—do I ever need this again? Archival for compliance

Let's suppose that you're designing infrastructure for an instant messaging application. You'll need lots of throughput for the transmission of fresh messages, but access to messages that are over a week old is rare. Compliance rules in some regions for these types of social applications, though, insist that all messages for all users are available for the prevention of misuse of the application. This means that there is a big data lake using up space on your live system that's not required for day-to-day operation. You might have something similar in your application: old products, old user profiles, and that sort of thing.

This sort of data should be archived. Whether or not this data is archived away from AWS is a decision that you need to make. If you need your users to still be able to access this data—it might only be that a few users access it a couple of times—then it should stay on AWS; otherwise, *off-site* storage might be more appropriate.

For this sort of data, Redshift or S3 Glacier would be appropriate candidates. They are both designed for long-term, low frequency access to the data stored therein, but provide the ability to query for it as necessary.

Sizing your storage

The size of your data storage capacity directly influences price. The more space you need for your data and the more frequently you need to access it, the more you need to pay: it's that simple. It makes sense to only provision what you need if you're using an EBS volume or if you're using the RDS. Relational storage can become expensive quickly if used inappropriately.

It can be difficult to plan the storage requirements for a project, particularly over the course of a long project. For large projects, or for projects where there are strict budget control requirements, periodic assessment of the amount of storage may be necessary to ensure that costs do not spiral and that the most efficient amount of storage is being used.

If you are using data services provided by AWS, such as DynamoDB or ElasticSearch, then charging starts when you've exceeded the free tier capacities. If you're still in development, or have a low capacity, then the free tier might be more than generous.

Streamed

Some data types, due to their size, benefit from being streamed to the client. AWS has services that cater for dedicated streaming of different sources of information—think media services. S3 can also be used as a stream source. However, you would need to initiate and handle the stream through your application to stream from there.

Compressed

Data or assets that can't be streamed should be compressed for transport to the requesting client.

Choices here seem to fall along two lines: compress the data/asset yourself prior to storage, or use CloudFront to compress resources for you. If using CloudFront, you will need to provide configuration for the types of data/assets that you require to be compressed. Your application or service would then request those assets with a correct HTTP header (`Accept-Encoding: gzip`).

Sparse data

Sparse data is any kind of discrete data packet that gets sent periodically from a non-IT device—think IoT, weather stations, and traffic cameras. This type of data usually describes things such as local humidity, temperature, how often something is used, whether/when something is moved, or how many things travel through a sensors field of vision: in essence, tracking rare events or changes in current conditions.

Storage of this data is usually not an issue; the issue arises when this data needs to be analyzed, trying to find patterns and correlations.

Slowly changing data

Data that changes slowly, or rarely, is a candidate for pre-loading into a cache for access on system built from a data file (or even directly from Terraform) and being kept in the cache with an artificially high timeout, or even indefinitely (for as long as the system is active). Management of this data becomes a cache maintenance issue, rather than a database storage/access and provisioning size issue.

This way, it can be accessed by your application, but you save yourself database round trips.

RDS

AWS has an RDS that is a wrapper that provides a number of different industry standard database engines. There are six engines provided:

- Amazon Aurora
- PostgreSQL
- MySQL
- MariaDB
- Oracle Database
- MS SQL Server

If you're using Aurora to hold your data, you have a further choice between Basic and MySQL-backed or PostgreSQL-backed. The decision around this is dependent on where the data is originally being held. Using Aurora has implications on data throughput speed, which might tip the balance in its favor: it is reportedly five times faster than MySQL and three times faster than PostgreSQL without requiring any application changes (`https://aws.amazon.com/rds/aurora/`). Additionally, as Aurora is part of RDS, there is no server overhead: it's all managed in the service.

AWS also provides a data migration service that automates the migration of data from your local relational database(s) to those in your infrastructure.

The next few sections will cover some basic concepts, culminating in discussing how to add Aurora to your infrastructure, before we move on to unstructured data.

Transactional data

If you are unfamiliar with databases, then you may not be aware of the following. Sometimes a change to the data of the database, or an addition to it, needs to happen in a reliable, guaranteed manner. If an error does occur, then all data changes need to be rolled back or removed. This guarantee is provided by a transaction.

In order to provide a transaction, a database must provide certain guarantees: Atomicity, Consistency, Isolation, and Durability, otherwise known as **ACID**.

There is an opposing database philosophy—BASE—that applies mainly to NoSQL-type database systems. **BASE** stands for **basic availability, soft state, and eventual consistency**, which is ideal for non-business critical data in distributed systems.

The database engines provided by AWS RDS support transactions and all provide ACID guarantees.

CAP Theorem

CAP Theorem describes how a distributed database system can only provide two out of three of the following concepts: high consistency, high availability, and partition tolerance.

CAP Theorem plays a significant role in Big Data as it helps organizations to decide which trade-offs to make to cater for their data use cases.

The following sections discuss these concepts.

High consistency

A system that displays high consistency is one where all of the nodes see the same data at the same time. What this means in practice is that any read operation will return the result of the most recent write operation regardless of which node is queried.

Any system has consistency if a write transaction starts from a consistent state and returns to a consistent state. Transactions can (and often do) shift systems into an inconsistent state, but if there is any issue with the transaction, then the entire operation is rolled back to the previous consistent state.

Nodes in the distributed system will still need time to update: nothing happens instantly, which has an impact on availability.

High availability

The availability of a system is a measure of the ability to submit requests to a system and get a non-error response (the request just needs to be successful; the system doesn't necessarily need to send the most recent write). To achieve high availability, a distributed system needs to be operational 100% of the time, whereby every client gets a response regardless of the state of any individual node.

Partition tolerance

Partition tolerance is the ability of a system to withstand node failure and still continue to operate, regardless of the number of messages available in the system between nodes. This is a measure of the data replication throughout the system across the nodes, ensuring that the system remains operational through intermittent node failure.

In reality, partition tolerance is a requirement for modern distributed systems, hence the trade-offs between different systems are usually a choice between consistency and availability.

Setting up Aurora and MySQL

How the databases are provisioned depends on which engine you want to use. If you want to use any of the Aurora engines, then you can use `aws_rds_cluster_instance`; otherwise, you'll need to use `aws_db_instance`.

Chapter 10

Setting up Aurora looks similar to this (which uses the default Aurora engine):

```
resource "aws_rds_cluster_instance" "cluster_instances" {
  count = 2
  identifier = "aurora-cluster-demo-${count.index}"
  cluster_identifier = "${aws_rds_cluster.default.id}"
  instance_class = "db.r4.large"
}

resource "aws_rds_cluster" "default" {
  cluster_identifier = "aurora-cluster-demo"
  availability_zones = ["us-west-2a", "us-west-2b", "us-west-2c"]
  database_name = "mydb"
  master_username = "foo"
  master_password = "barbut8chars"
}
```

Setting up for MySQL works as follows:

```
resource "aws_db_instance" "default" {
  allocated_storage = 20
  storage_type = "gp2"
  engine = "mysql"
  engine_version = "5.7"
  instance_class = "db.t2.micro"
  name = "mydb"
  username = "foo"
  password = "foobarbaz"
  parameter_group_name = "default.mysql5.7"
}
```

With this set up now, you will have AWS Aurora or MySQL in your infrastructure.

Refer to the following documentation, which can help you to use the automated monitoring tools to watch RDS and report when something is wrong: `https://docs.amazonaws.cn/en_us/AmazonRDS/latest/UserGuide/MonitoringOverview.html`.

[171]

Unstructured data

It doesn't always make sense to structure your data in a relational way. In many cases, it makes more sense to maintain data as either key-value mappings or in simple objects, or documents as a complete record. This data—or maybe information—is usually stored in one of the growing number of NoSQL datastores. NoSQL—meaning Not only SQL, rather than No SQL—is a catch-all term that covers document stores, key-value stores, and graph databases. Some of the most well known are as follows:

- Document datastores. Examples include the following:
    - MongoDB
    - CouchDB
- Key-value stores. The following is an example:
    - Redis
- Graph databases. Examples include the following:
    - Neo4j
    - Orion

AWS provides two document stores: DocumentDB and DynamoDB (which also acts as a key-value store) and the Neptune graph database.

The following sections will discuss how to use DynamoDB.

DynamoDB

Some of the world's largest-scale applications are supported by DynamoDB; it provides consistent, single-digit millisecond response times at all levels. It also allows us to build applications with virtually unlimited throughput and storage. DynamoDB global tables enable replication of your data across multiple AWS Regions. This hence gives you quick and local access to data for your applications that are distributed globally.

With DynamoDB being a managed service, it can auto-scale and has fault tolerance built-in.

ACID transactions will help you to build business-critical applications at any scale. All data is encrypted by DynamoDB by default. It also provides fine-grained identity and access control for all tables.

Setting DynamoDB up is just a case of creating a local table (and access policies), shown as follows:

```
resource "aws_dynamodb_table" "basic-dynamodb-table" {
  name = "ESName"
  billing_mode = "PROVISIONED"
  read_capacity = 20
  write_capacity = 20
  hash_key = "key"
  range_key = "range_key"

  attribute [
    ... attribute objects ...
  ]

  ttl {
    attribute_name = "TimeToExist"
    enabled = false
  }
}
```

Or you can add the table into the global space, as shown in the following code block:

```
resource "aws_dynamodb_table" "us-east-1" {
  provider - "aws.us-east-1"

  hash_key = "myAttribute"
  name = "myTable"
  stream_enabled = true
  stream_view_type = "NEW_AND_OLD_IMAGES"
  read_capacity = 1
  write_capacity = 1

  attribute {
    name = "myAttribute"
    type = "S"
  }
}

resource "aws_dynamodb_global_table" "myTable" {
  depends_on = ["aws_dynamodb_table.us-east-1", "aws_dynamodb_table.us-west-2"]
  provider = "aws.us-east-1"

  name = "myTable"

  replica {
    region_name = "us-east-1"
```

```
  }
  replica {
    region_name = "us-west-2"
  }
}
```

Global tables are layered on top of local ones and can be made multi-regional.

With relational data services covered, you'll now discover other forms of persistence that you can use in your AWS infrastructure.

Polyglot persistence

Sometimes, it might not be appropriate, or you might not want, to manage your data purely in a relational database: there might be advantages to having some of it denormalized into documents or added to a search index. Your data might just be a simple mapping between an identifier and a value (key-value), or something else entirely. This mash-up of different storage types dependent on usage or data types is called **polyglot persistence**.

AWS provides many different data storage types. Most are managed services and have the capabilities and guarantees associated with them being managed services.

In particular, you'll look at the following:

- ElasticSearch
- CloudTrail
- Elemental MediaStore
- EMR
- Neptune
- Timestream

Text

Many storage engines store, index, and analyze textual, binary, and log data. This section covers some of the catalog provided by AWS to handle various data sources and how to create them.

ElasticSearch

ElasticSearch is a search engine. It is based on Apache Lucene, a popular open source project. ElasticSearch stores data in indexes. Access to the data contained within ElasticSearch is provided by REST API.

Setting up an ElasticSearch cluster takes a little bit of patience as there are a few parts to define.

First, we need to add a domain. Here, we're also adding in encryption to protect data:

```
resource "aws_elasticsearch_domain" "es" {
  domain_name = "my-es-domain"
  elasticsearch_version = "7.2"

  encrypt_at_rest {
    enabled = true
  }

  node_to_node_encryption {
    enabled = true
  }
}
```

Add into this definition additional elements, including any CloudWatch log groups:

```
advanced_options {
  "rest.action.multi.allow_explicit_index" = "true"
}

cluster_config {
  instance_count = "1"
  instance_type = "c4.large.elasticsearch"
  zone_awareness_enabled = true
}

ebs_options {
  ebs_enabled = true
  volume_size = "10"
}

snapshot_options {
  automated_snapshot_start_hour = "0"
}

log_publishing_options {
  log_type = "INDEX_SLOW_LOGS"
  cloudwatch_log_group_arn = "${aws_cloudwatch_log_group.es-slow-index-
```

```
    logs.arn}"
      enabled = true
  }

  depends_on = [
    ... log dependencies ...
  ]

  tags {
    "Workspace" = "es-tag"
    "Terraform" = true
  }
```

Make sure that you've set the log groups in the `depends_on` section; that way, you make sure that the logs are up and running before the ElasticSearch.

CloudTrail

CloudTrail provides metrics for usage of your infrastructure. It monitors and logs the activity across your AWS account, creating audit trails (both operational and risk) and governance and ensuring compliance by keeping track of events from the command console, SDK, CLI, and other services.

To use CloudTrail, you need a service account, created as follows:

```
data "aws_cloudtrail_service_account" "main" {}

resource "aws_s3_bucket" "bucket" {
  bucket = "tf-cloudtrail-logging-test-bucket"
  force_destroy = true

  policy = <<EOF
{
  "Version": "2008-10-17",
  "Statement": [
    {
      "Sid": "Put bucket policy needed for trails",
      "Effect": "Allow",
      "Principal": {
        "AWS": "${data.aws_cloudtrail_service_account.main.arn}"
      },
      "Action": "s3:PutObject",
      "Resource": "arn:aws:s3:::tf-cloudtrail-logging-test-bucket/*"
    },
    {
      "Sid": "Get bucket policy needed for trails",
```

```
      "Effect": "Allow",
      "Principal": {
        "AWS": "${data.aws_cloudtrail_service_account.main.arn}"
      },
      "Action": "s3:GetBucketAcl",
      "Resource": "arn:aws:s3:::tf-cloudtrail-logging-test-bucket"
    }
  ]
}
EOF
}
```

Once that's in place, you will also need to set up which parts of your infrastructure you want to monitor, using a resource definition similar to the following:

```
resource "aws_cloudtrail" "example" {
  # ... other configuration ...

  event_selector {
    read_write_type = "All"
    include_management_events = true

    data_resource {
      type = "AWS::S3::Object"

      # Make sure to append a trailing '/' to your ARN if you want
      # to monitor all objects in a bucket.
      values = ["${data.aws_s3_bucket.important-bucket.arn}/"]
    }
  }
}
```

And there you have it: CloudTrail is in your infrastructure.

> Many more options are available, so be sure to check the documentation at: https://www.terraform.io/docs/providers/aws/r/cloudtrail.html.

Elemental MediaStore—dedicated services for video

Elemental MediaStore is a storage service optimized for media files. It gives you the performance, consistency, and low latency required to deliver live streaming video content.

Elemental MediaStore can act as the store in your video workflow. Its high performance capabilities meet the needs of the most demanding media delivery workloads.

MediaStore requires a container as follows:

```
resource "aws_media_store_container" "example" {
  name = "example"
}
```

And it contains a policy document:

```
resource "aws_media_store_container_policy" "example" {
  container_name = "${aws_media_store_container.example.name}"

  policy = <<EOF
{
    "Version": "2012-10-17",
    "Statement": [{
        "Sid": "MediaStoreFullAccess",
        "Action": [ "mediastore:*" ],
        "Principal": {"AWS" : "arn:aws:iam::${data.aws_caller_identity.current.account_id}:root"},
        "Effect": "Allow",
        "Resource": "arn:aws:mediastore:${data.aws_caller_identity.current.account_id}:${data.aws_region.current.name}:container/${aws_media_store_container.example.name}/*",
        "Condition": {
            "Bool": { "aws:SecureTransport": "true" }
        }
    }]
}
EOF
}
```

Combined, these two listings lay out the creation of a MediaStore.

S3 – binary files

Binary files (for example, audio files) are best stored in **Simple Storage Service** or **S3**. S3 is an object storage service that offers leading availability, resilience, scalability, and performance.

Setting up an S3 bucket is simple and has been covered several times. As a reminder, look at the following code:

```
data "aws_s3_bucket" "selected" {
  bucket = "bucket.test.com"
}

data "aws_route53_zone" "test_zone" {
  name = "test.com."
}

resource "aws_route53_record" "example" {
  zone_id = "${data.aws_route53_zone.test_zone.id}"
  name = "bucket"
  type = "A"

  alias {
    name = "${data.aws_s3_bucket.selected.website_domain}"
    zone_id = "${data.aws_s3_bucket.selected.hosted_zone_id}"
  }
}
```

Setting up S3 buckets should be run-of-the-mill stuff by now.

EMR

EMR is a Hadoop-powered managed service that's easy, fast, and cost-effective at processing vast amounts of data across dynamically scalable EC2 instances.

EMR is also capable of running other distributed frameworks, such as Apache Spark, HBase, Presto, and Flink. It securely and reliably handles a broad set of big data use cases, including log analysis, web indexing, data transformations (ETL), machine learning, financial analysis, scientific simulation, and bioinformatics.

Setting up EMR is a case of creating a cluster, shown as follows:

```
resource "aws_emr_cluster" "cluster" {
  name = "emr-test-arn"
  release_label = "emr-4.6.0"
  applications = ["Hadoop"]
  termination_protection = false
  keep_job_flow_alive_when_no_steps = true

  ec2_attributes {
    subnet_id = "${aws_subnet.main.id}"
    emr_managed_master_security_group = "${aws_security_group.sg.id}"
```

```
    emr_managed_slave_security_group = "${aws_security_group.sg.id}"
    instance_profile = "${aws_iam_instance_profile.emr_profile.arn}"
  }

  instance_group {
    instance_role = "CORE"
    instance_type = "c4.large"
    instance_count = "1"
    ebs_config {
      size = "40"
      type = "gp2"
      volumes_per_instance = 1
    }
    bid_price = "0.30"
    autoscaling_policy = <<EOF
{
"Constraints": {
  "MinCapacity": 1,
  "MaxCapacity": 2
},
"Rules": [
  ... Add required rules here ...
]
}
EOF
  }
  ebs_root_volume_size = 100

  master_instance_type = "m5.xlarge"
  core_instance_type = "m5.xlarge"
  core_instance_count = 1

  bootstrap_action {
    path = "s3://elasticmapreduce/bootstrap-actions/run-if"
    name = "runif"
    args = ["instance.isMaster=true", "echo running on master node"]
  }

  configurations_json = <<EOF
  [
    ... Environment configurations here ...
  ]
EOF
  service_role = "${aws_iam_role.iam_emr_service_role.arn}"
}
```

That's a long list, but as you can see, it's doing a lot of stuff. You need to set up the type of application you can run on the EMR, and which attributes, rules, and constraints it needs to operate under. It also specifies the size of the cluster instance that you want to run it on.

Graph databases

Graph databases are designed to treat the connections (relationships) between data with equal importance as the data itself. They hold data without constricting it to a pre-defined schema; instead, the data is stored in a way that shows how each individual entity is connected with or related to all of the others.

These database engines have advantages over relational databases for several use cases, such as social networks, recommendation engines, and fraud detection where the relationships between the data are as important as the data itself. The challenges of building these sorts of data structures with relational databases mean the joining of multiple tables with multiple foreign keys, using SQL that requires nested queries, and complex joins that can quickly become unwieldy and unmaintainable. These sorts of queries do not perform well over large datasets.

Neptune

Neptune is a fully managed service that is highly available and has the capability to continuously back up to S3. It is also secure as data is encrypted.

Neptune uses graph structures such as nodes and edges alongside properties to represent data. Relationships are first-order citizens within the model, which allows the data to be directly linked—this improves query performance.

In order to use Neptune, you need to create a cluster and a cluster instance:

```
resource "aws_neptune_cluster" "default" {
  cluster_identifier = "neptune-cluster-demo"
  engine = "neptune"
  backup_retention_period = 5
  preferred_backup_window = "07:00-09:00"
  skip_final_snapshot = true
  iam_database_authentication_enabled = "true"
  apply_immediately = "true"
}

resource "aws_neptune_cluster_instance" "example" {
  count = 1
  cluster_identifier = "${aws_neptune_cluster.default.id}"
```

```
    engine = "neptune"
    instance_class = "db.r4.large"
    apply_immediately = "true"
}
```

With an instance in place, you can optionally add topics and event subscriptions, as demonstrated as follows:

```
resource "aws_sns_topic" "default" {
  name = "neptune-events"
}

resource "aws_neptune_event_subscription" "default" {
  name = "neptune-event-sub"
  sns_topic_arn = "${aws_sns_topic.default.arn}"

  source_type = "db-instance"
  source_ids = ["${aws_neptune_cluster_instance.example.id}"]

  event_categories = [
    "maintenance",
    "availability",
    "creation",
    "backup",
    "restoration",
    "recovery",
    "deletion",
    "failover",
    "failure",
    "notification",
    "configuration change",
    "read replica",
  ]

  tags = {
    "env" = "test"
  }
}
```

Here, you can see how to set up subscriptions for your Neptune instance, listing the events that are expected to be received.

Time series

Processing data over time is one of the growing use cases for IoT applications: being able to understand how events from devices change over time. Relational databases can store this data, but because they lack various optimizations, are unable to analyze this data efficiently by time series and it becomes costly to analyze this data.

Time series data has certain characteristics such as the fact that it arrives in time order form and is append-only and queries occur over a time interval.

Amazon purposely built Timestream to handle this sort of data: to be able to store and process data by time interval.

Timestream

Timestream provides an adaptive query engine that can be made to understand your data, which in turn simplifies your data and increases the speed at which it is analyzed.

Timestream comes with the following advantages:

- It's serverless: so there's no time-consuming infrastructure provisioning or patching.
- It automates standard data tasks: rollups, retention, compression, and tiering.
- It processes data quickly at low cost: it's x1,000 times faster than RDS engines at 1/10 of the cost.
- Distributed and parallel: inserts and queries occur on different tiers reducing contention.

At this point in time, Timestream is only available for preview and can only be set up through the AWS command console. Be advised that this is cutting edge technology and specifics are not currently available. Once this service is available on general release, it will be a game changer for many applications that require real-time data analysis.

Summary

As you can see, the options for data storage, access, and analysis are legion. There are solutions to cater for all of your needs.

How you segment and store your data is highly dependent on its use case. Not every project will need a search index or relational database, but they are easily reachable if you need them. Be mindful that services come at a cost and that misuse of the services is likely to end up in an expensive bill each month. Experimentation to determine the best use of services will pay dividends, not only in budgetary terms, but in terms of speed of data access and the responsiveness of your application.

This chapter covered various aspects of persistence services provided by AWS. The next chapter will discuss various techniques for processing the data in your infrastructure, especially in the field of machine learning.

Further reading

To read further on the differences between ACID and BASE database types, see: `https://neo4j.com/blog/acid-vs-base-consistency-models-explained/`.

11
Data Processing - Handling Your Data Transformation

In this chapter, we will discuss patterns for batch and stream processing, queuing chains, priority queues, and job observers. AWS has many tools to make much of this simple and to remove many potential issues encountered in trying to manage and scale these services.

We will investigate dynamic data patterns such as state sharing, URL rewriting, rewrite/cache proxying, data replication, in-memory caching, and sharding. Identifying appropriate constructs for handling data, designing appropriate intervals for data collection, detecting meaningful patterns in events, and understanding how to share information across instances are the main highlights of this chapter.

The following topics will be covered in this chapter in brief:

- Queueing
- Batching
- Caching
- Event stream processing
- Machine learning

Queuing

Queues are used to collect intra-system messages and/or external events. Processing of these messages can happen sequentially or in parallel, depending on how many consumers are available to process them. Messages can also be routed to different parts of your system based on various criteria (as dictated by the queuing engine), to make sure that it is handled appropriately.

AWS provides different queues and queue-like services for different purposes:

- **Managed Streaming for Kafka (MSK)**
- Kinesis (data streams and firehose)
- Amazon MQ
- Amazon **Simple Queue Service (SQS)**

We will be discussing Kafka in this section.

MSK

MSK is a managed service. Apache Kafka is a platform for building real-time streaming pipelines that can be used to populate data lakes, stream system changes, and events, moving data to and from databases. Machine learning and analytics applications can also benefit from using MSK.

There is usually a significant challenge in setting up Kafka clusters; using MSK saves you from having to do this yourself and from the additional management issues that can arise from running a distributed queuing system.

Setting this up looks similar to Terraform as follows:

```
resource "aws_msk_cluster" "example_cluster" {
  name = "example-name"
  client_subnets = [
    "example-subnet-1",
    "example-subnet-2"
  ]
  broker_count = 1
  broker_instance_type = "kafka.m5.large"
  broker_security_groups = [
    "example-security-group-1"
  ]
  broker_volume_size = 2
  kafka_version = "2.12"
}
```

This Terraform is currently at the cutting edge and waiting for final sign-offs. By the time this book is available, this should be available as standard functionality.

Batching

Sometimes, your data sources produce too much data to process, the operation that you want to use over the data uses is too intensive to process on collection, or you need to analyze data but it doesn't need to be in *real time* (whatever that means for your application). In order to process this data effectively, it needs to happen away from the action, so to speak, in a remote system or at an off-peak time. Batch processing happens periodically.

Batch processing is a useful tool in the arsenal of data scientists, developers, and engineers. Being able to process large amounts of data for further analysis or for presentation to business users without overloading your application services or databases allows you to schedule and execute your analysis patterns across a number of AWS services.

In order to set this service up, perform the following steps:

1. Create an IAM role and security group:

    ```
    resource "aws_iam_role" "ecs_instance_role" {
      name = "ecs_instance_role"

      assume_role_policy = <<EOF
    {
        "Version": "2012-10-17",
        "Statement": [
        {
            "Action": "sts:AssumeRole",
            "Effect": "Allow",
            "Principal": {
            "Service": "ec2.amazonaws.com"
            }
        }
        ]
    }
    EOF
    }

    resource "aws_iam_role_policy_attachment" "ecs_instance_role" {
      role       = "${aws_iam_role.ecs_instance_role.name}"
      policy_arn = "arn:aws:iam::aws:policy/service-role/AmazonEC2ContainerServiceforEC2Role"
    }

    resource "aws_iam_instance_profile" "ecs_instance_role" {
      name = "ecs_instance_role"
      role = "${aws_iam_role.ecs_instance_role.name}"
    ```

```
}

resource "aws_iam_role" "aws_batch_service_role" {
  name = "aws_batch_service_role"

  assume_role_policy = <<EOF
{
    "Version": "2012-10-17",
    "Statement": [
    {
        "Action": "sts:AssumeRole",
        "Effect": "Allow",
        "Principal": {
        "Service": "batch.amazonaws.com"
        }
    }
    ]
}
EOF
}

resource "aws_iam_role_policy_attachment" "aws_batch_service_role"
{
  role = "${aws_iam_role.aws_batch_service_role.name}"
  policy_arn = "arn:aws:iam::aws:policy/service-role/AWSBatchServiceRole"
}

resource "aws_security_group" "sample" {
  name = "aws_batch_compute_environment_security_group"
}
```

2. You will also need to set up a VPC in order to house the batch processing:

```
resource "aws_vpc" "sample" {
  cidr_block = "10.1.0.0/16"
}

resource "aws_subnet" "sample" {
  vpc_id = "${aws_vpc.sample.id}"
  cidr_block = "10.1.1.0/24"
}
```

3. With all of these pieces in place, we link them all together into a batch computing environment:

```
resource "aws_batch_compute_environment" "sample" {
  compute_environment_name = "sample"

  compute_resources {
    instance_role = "${aws_iam_instance_profile.ecs_instance_role.arn}"

    instance_type = [
      "c4.large",
    ]

    max_vcpus = 16
    min_vcpus = 0

    security_group_ids = [
      "${aws_security_group.sample.id}",
    ]

    subnets = [
      "${aws_subnet.sample.id}",
    ]
    type = "EC2"
  }

  service_role = "${aws_iam_role.aws_batch_service_role.arn}"
  type = "MANAGED"
  depends_on = ["aws_iam_role_policy_attachment.aws_batch_service_role"]
}
```

4. You can add job queues to this environment,:

```
resource "aws_batch_job_queue" "test_queue" {
  name = "tf-test-batch-job-queue"
  state = "ENABLED"
  priority = 1
  compute_environments = [
    "${aws_batch_compute_environment.test_environment_1.arn}",
    "${aws_batch_compute_environment.test_environment_2.arn}",
  ]
}
```

Data Processing - Handling Your Data Transformation

5. You can also create containers for batch execution of individual jobs:

```
resource "aws_batch_job_definition" "test" {
  name = "tf_test_batch_job_definition"
  type = "container"

  container_properties = <<CONTAINER_PROPERTIES
{
    "command": ["ls", "-la"],
    "image": "busybox",
    "memory": 1024,
    "vcpus": 1,
    "volumes": [
      {
        "host": {
          "sourcePath": "/tmp"
        },
        "name": "tmp"
      }
    ],
    "environment": [
        {"name": "VARNAME", "value": "VARVAL"}
    ],
    "mountPoints": [
        {
          "sourceVolume": "tmp",
          "containerPath": "/tmp",
          "readOnly": false
        }
    ],
    "ulimits": [
      {
        "hardLimit": 1024,
        "name": "nofile",
        "softLimit": 1024
      }
    ]
}
CONTAINER_PROPERTIES
}
```

Batch processing is only one way of processing large datasets in manageable chunks. An alternative is stream processing, which is covered later in this chapter, but first, we'll take a look at caching.

Caching

Caching is used to temporarily store data that is frequently requested in an in-memory data store with low latency access, reducing round-trip access to the primary application data store(s). This makes retrieving cached data far quicker.

Caching is usually, but not necessarily, transient. This means that periodically, the data expires and needs to be rebuilt, but at a much reduced cost compared to continuously querying for the data from the data stores.

ElastiCache

ElastiCache is a fully managed service that provides Redis and Memcache. With ElastiCache, you can deploy, run, and scale these services. This helps you to build data-intensive apps or to add caching capability to your application using these in-memory data stores.

Using ElastiCache, you can create a managed cluster with all of the properties of a managed service:

```
resource "aws_elasticache_cluster" "example" {
  cluster_id = "cluster-example"
  engine = "memcached"
  replication_group_id = "${aws_elasticache_replication_group.example.id}"
}
```

This can be linked to a replication group that can span multiple availability zones:

```
resource "aws_elasticache_replication_group" "example" {
  automatic_failover_enabled = true
  availability_zones = ["us-west-2a", "us-west-2b"]
  replication_group_id = "tf-rep-group-1"
  replication_group_description = "test description"
  node_type = "cache.m4.large"
  number_cache_clusters = 2
  parameter_group_name = "default.memcached1.4"
  port = 112211
}
```

Data caching is for when data has been processed and is being used: it's for output. You also need to understand how to handle input; that's being covered in the following sections.

Event stream processing

Event stream processing can happen in a number of ways on AWS. One of the ways—Kinesis—we will cover separately. We will discuss using Elastic MapReduce here.

Elastic MapReduce is capable of using several different types of processing engines: Hadoop, Apache Spark, HBase, Presto, and Apache Flink. All of these engines are used for processing large amounts of data: some, such as Spark and Flink, are for real-time data processing, and Hadoop is for batch processing and so much more.

Standard EMR has already been covered in a previous chapter.

Using Flink (or another engine) via Terraform is as easy as changing the application's array content, as shown in the following block:

```
resource "aws_emr_cluster" "cluster" {
  name = "emr-test-arn"
  release_label = "emr-4.6.0"
  applications = ["Flink"]
  additional_info = <<EOF
{
  "instanceAwsClientConfiguration": {
    "proxyPort": 8099,
    "proxyHost": "myproxy.example.com"
  }
}
EOF
```

Next, set the correct configuration details in the configuration element of the same resource configuration:

```
configurations_json = <<EOF
    [
      {
        "Classification": "flink-env",
        "Configurations": [
          {
            "Classification": "export",
            "Properties": {
              "JAVA_HOME": "/usr/lib/jvm/java-1.8.0"
            }
          }
        ],
        "Properties": {}
      }
    ]
EOF
```

EMR is a generalized event processing system that processes data in real time. Once, it's processed and persisted (the assumption here is S3), you could find yourself needing to query it to find more useful information. This is where Athena (the subject of the next section), comes in.

Athena (querying S3)

Athena is a service that allows you to query the data stored in S3 by providing a schema and using standards-compliant SQL. Typically, response times are in the order of seconds, due to the type and amount of data that is being queried; however, as the syntax is SQL, there is no need for complex **ETL**—which stands for **extract, transform, load**—to prepare results:

```
resource "aws_athena_database" "hoge" {
  name = "users"
  bucket = "${aws_s3_bucket.hoge.bucket}"
}

resource "aws_athena_named_query" "foo" {
  name = "bar"
  database = "${aws_athena_database.hoge.name}"
  query = "SELECT * FROM ${aws_athena_database.hoge.name} limit 10;"
}
```

Athena uses Presto, which is custom-built by Amazon for use in multiple services. Presto provides ANSI SQL support to Athena, but that support also extends to working with a number of standard data formats such as CSV and JSON.

Athena is a managed service with the ability to execute queries across availability regions and, with S3, it becomes highly available.

The Athena engine can be used to make general queries, but it also has the capability to efficiently handle complex queries, including large joins, window functions, and arrays/matrices, and it provides standard tooling for in-depth data analysis.

Transforms

Data sources often don't provide useful forms of information. Data and information are two different things. Data needs to be processed into useful forms: information. This sort of processing in traditional setups is usually a process such as ETL, but can also cover encoding changes for media files, **natural language processing** (**NLP**), or data mining.

Transforms are a natural part of processing data and should be an integral part of your data processing pipeline.

Audio/video (mp4 to mp3)

Elemental MediaConvert is a video transcoding service that can also broadcast. This video-on-demand service allows for broadcasting to multiscreen devices at whatever scale you need. Both audio and video are served by this service using a simple web interface.

Setting up MediaConvert is not currently available using Terraform and can only currently be set up using the API or the AWS Console. This looks to be due to change at some point in the future though, so it pays to keep tabs on the Terraform documentation.

Elastic Transcoder

Elastic Transcoder is media transcoding in the cloud. It is designed to be highly scalable and easy to use for developers and businesses to transcode media files from their source format into versions that will play back on multiple device types.

Elastic Transcoder works using a pipeline and it requires an S3 bucket and an IAM role, as shown in the following example:

```
resource "aws_elastictranscoder_pipeline" "bar" {
  input_bucket = "${aws_s3_bucket.input_bucket.bucket}"
  name = "aws_elastictranscoder_pipeline_tf_test_"
  role = "${aws_iam_role.test_role.arn}"

  content_config {
    bucket = "${aws_s3_bucket.content_bucket.bucket}"
    storage_class = "Standard"
  }

  thumbnail_config {
    bucket = "${aws_s3_bucket.thumb_bucket.bucket}"
    storage_class = "Standard"
  }
}
```

You can also set up various preset transcoders to assist with handling of media files. This is done as shown in the following example:

```
resource "aws_elastictranscoder_preset" "bar" {
  container = "mp4"
  description = "Sample Preset"
  name = "sample_preset"

  audio {
    audio_packing_mode = "SingleTrack"
    bit_rate = 96
    channels = 2
    codec = "AAC"
    sample_rate = 44100
  }

  audio_codec_options {
    profile = "AAC-LC"
  }

  video {
    bit_rate = "1600"
    codec = "H.264"
    display_aspect_ratio = "16:9"
    fixed_gop = "false"
    frame_rate = "auto"
    max_frame_rate = "60"
    keyframes_max_dist = 240
    max_height = "auto"
    max_width = "auto"
    padding_policy = "Pad"
    sizing_policy = "Fit"
  }

  video_codec_options = {
    Profile = "main"
    Level = "2.2"
    MaxReferenceFrames = 3
    InterlacedMode = "Progressive"
    ColorSpaceConversionMode = "None"
  }

  video_watermarks {
    id = "Terraform Test"
    max_width = "20%"
    max_height = "20%"
    sizing_policy = "ShrinkToFit"
    horizontal_align = "Right"
```

Data Processing - Handling Your Data Transformation

```
      horizontal_offset = "10px"
      vertical_align = "Bottom"
      vertical_offset = "10px"
      opacity = "55.5"
      target = "Content"
    }

    thumbnails {
      format = "png"
      interval = 120
      max_width = "auto"
      max_height = "auto"
      padding_policy = "Pad"
      sizing_policy = "Fit"
    }
  }
```

Media transcoders are one thing, but handling events and messages at scale—that's a job for Kinesis, which is covered next.

Kinesis

Kinesis is a streaming data service that allows for collection, processing, and real-time analysis of data to allow you to gain insights into new information to enable your organization to react appropriately. Kinesis can handle textual data, web events, audio/video data, application and web log data, IoT events, machine learning, and analytics.

This is a real-time data processor to get initial information from the data stream. After this initial information, the data can be pushed into a data lake and then batch processed.

Setting up a Kinesis stream for data analysis requires a prior Kinesis stream to be able to hook the analysis engine. Setting up a stream is as follows:

```
    resource "aws_kinesis_stream" "test_stream" {
      name = "terraform-kinesis-test"
      shard_count = 1
      retention_period = 48

      shard_level_metrics = [
        "IncomingBytes",
        "OutgoingBytes",
      ]

      tags = {
```

```
      Environment = "test"
    }
}
```

With the stream in place, you can attach it to a stream processor, as follows:

```
resource "aws_kinesis_stream" "test_stream" {
  name = "terraform-kinesis-test"
  shard_count = 1
}

resource "aws_kinesis_analytics_application" "test_application" {
  name = "kinesis-analytics-application-test"

  inputs {
    name_prefix = "test_prefix"
    kinesis_stream {
      resource_arn = "${aws_kinesis_stream.test_stream.arn}"
      role_arn = "${aws_iam_role.test.arn}"
    }
    parallelism {
      count = 1
    }
    schema {
      record_columns {
        mapping = "$.test"
        name = "test"
        sql_type = "VARCHAR(8)"
      }
      record_encoding = "UTF-8"
      record_format {
        mapping_parameters {
          json {
            record_row_path = "$"
          }
        }
      }
    }
  }
}
```

Kinesis is a streaming service with multiple alternatives for handling and transforming data. Next, we'll look at how AWS facilitates data collection across your AWS estate.

CloudTrail

AWS provides a service that manages project governance, compliance, operational, and risk auditing of your account—this service is CloudTrail. With CloudTrail, you can continuously log and monitor account activity and analyze usage patterns across your infrastructure: you can see event histories from management console access, command-line tools, APIs, SDKs, and other related services. This comprehensive auditing tool makes security order, change tracking, and issue resolution simpler.

CloudTrail is simple enough to set up using Terraform: all you need to do is attach it to an S3 bucket with a relevant access policy, as shown in the following example:

```
resource "aws_cloudtrail" "foobar" {
  name = "tf-trail-foobar"
  s3_bucket_name = "${aws_s3_bucket.foo.id}"
  s3_key_prefix = "prefix"
  include_global_service_events = false
}

resource "aws_s3_bucket" "foo" {
  bucket = "tf-test-trail"
  force_destroy = true

  policy = <<POLICY
{
    "Version": "2012-10-17",
    "Statement": [
        {
            "Sid": "AWSCloudTrailAclCheck",
            "Effect": "Allow",
            "Principal": {
              "Service": "cloudtrail.amazonaws.com"
            },
            "Action": "s3:GetBucketAcl",
            "Resource": "arn:aws:s3:::tf-test-trail"
        },
        {
            "Sid": "AWSCloudTrailWrite",
            "Effect": "Allow",
            "Principal": {
              "Service": "cloudtrail.amazonaws.com"
            },
            "Action": "s3:PutObject",
            "Resource": "arn:aws:s3:::tf-test-trail/*",
            "Condition": {
                "StringEquals": {
                    "s3:x-amz-acl": "bucket-owner-full-control"
```

```
                    }
                }
            }
        ]
    }
POLICY
}
```

With these different transformation engines explored, we'll start discovering machine learning and its support in AWS.

Machine learning

Being able to anticipate your customers' needs, or find patterns across your data, are growth areas for businesses right now—this type of business intelligence is currently the holy grail. Being able to design and train **Artificial Intelligence** (**AI**) to find patterns and connections in your data lake gives the users of your application a better experience.

This section covers the various tools and concepts for machine learning and AI available for AWS customers.

In particular, you will discover these two tools:

- Amazon SageMaker
- Amazon Comprehend

And we will cover the concepts of the following:

- AI
- Anomaly detection
- Prediction
- Forecasting

Amazon SageMaker

SageMaker can be used to build, train, and deploy machine learning models quickly. As a fully managed service, it covers the entire workflow: labeling and preparing data; choosing and training an algorithm; tuning and optimizing for deployment; making predictions; and taking actions.

To set up SageMaker, you first need to create a model to hold your data. The model requires some privileges, so you'll need to set up an IAM role too:

```
resource "aws_sagemaker_model" "m" {
    name = "my-model"
    execution_role_arn = "${aws_iam_role.foo.arn}"

    primary_container {
        image = "174872318107.dkr.ecr.us-west-2.amazonaws.com/kmeans:1"
    }
}

resource "aws_iam_role" "r" {
  assume_role_policy = "${data.aws_iam_policy_document.assume_role.json}"
}

data "aws_iam_policy_document" "assume_role" {
  statement {
    actions = [ "sts:AssumeRole" ]
    principals {
      type = "Service"
      identifiers = [ "sagemaker.amazonaws.com" ]
    }
  }
}
```

With this in place, you can set up configuration for your endpoint. Configuration comes first, as it links the endpoint to the model:

```
resource "aws_sagemaker_endpoint_configuration" "ec" {
    name = "my-endpoint-config"

    production_variant {
        variant_name = "variant-1"
        model_name = "${aws_sagemaker_model.m.name}"
        initial_instance_count = 1
        instance_type = "ml.t2.medium"
    }

    tags {
        Name = "foo"
    }
}
```

Finally, here is the endpoint, which is relatively simple in comparison:

```
resource "aws_sagemaker_endpoint" "e" {
    name = "my-endpoint"
    endpoint_config_name =
"${aws_sagemaker_endpoint_configuration.ec.name}"

    tags = {
      Name = "foo"
    }
}
```

All of this sets up SageMaker ready for population.

Jupyter Notebook

Jupyter Notebook is fast becoming the standard for sharing information obtained from big data processing. It is a web application that allows management of notebook documents.

Setting up Jupyter is outside of Terraform, but simply put, you need to do the following:

1. Install and configure the Jupyter Notebook server on an EC2 instance.
2. Configure your local client to access the Jupyter Notebook server.

For more information about Jupyter Notebook, see `https://jupyter.org/`.

Amazon Comprehend – NLP

Your unstructured data contains a huge amount of information: probably more than you realize. The information contained in emails and other feedback from customers, support requests, reviews, social media interchanges, and other sources of customer data can provide further insight into business improvements that cater for a better customer experience. This is where machine learning and NLP comes in: in order to analyze this data, these paradigms can be used to translate all of this customer data into interesting items that can be used for improved business responses.

Comprehend uses machine learning techniques to uncover relationships in your unstructured data. This service tokenizes the text in the data as per NLP techniques to parse elements to identify the key phrases, places, people, brands, events, and topics contained therein. It also understands the context in which the analyzed information is embedded. The relevance of this data to your data analysis and customer feedback teams can be determined using Comprehend's AutoML facility to build custom entities or classifications.

Comprehend has specialist services for identifying medical terms (things such as conditions, medications, dosages, and strengths) and multiple languages from the unstructured data. Comprehend Medical can also be used to identify relationships between different medical data sources to match medications and tests, treatments, and procedures.

There is currently no Terraform script to create Comprehend resources, but there are some projects on GitHub that provide access to build these services via build scripts.

AI

AI is a computer science field that tries to solve problems based on human cognition and intelligence using computer models to simulate human traits such as the ability to learn, recognize patterns, and solve problems.

When creating—or, rather, training—AI or machine learning models, the techniques used fall into two broad categories: those that are supervised and those that are unsupervised. Supervised training models are those that also provide the expected outcome data in the available dataset. This ensures that the model can iteratively train itself to achieve the outcomes provided.

In the same vein, being able to supply a sufficiently large pool of training data means that you can train your AI faster and make it smarter or more accurate. Every day, your business is creating a pool of data that you can use to train your ML or DL engines—this data can be pulled from a data lake (think Redshift) and then normalized or mined through a number of AWS services.

From the work of Pedro Domingo (The Master Algorithm), AI models are thought to fit into one of five areas (or, as noted in the text, *tribes*), where certain advances in particular tribes (noted further on) have helped to propel both machine learning and deep learning as fields in their own right. Whilst the names for these areas might be different depending on which publications you've come across, the central tenant of each is fairly well defined. Here, they are understood to be the following:

- **Symbolists**: Models that are rooted in logic and philosophy
- **Connectionists**: Models that are used in neuroscience for deep learning
- **Evolutionaries**: Stems from models based on biological processes
- **Bayesians**: Statistics- and probability-based modelling for machine learning
- **Analogizers**: Models that are based on psychology

Anomaly detection

ML (or, for that matter, DL) can be used to determine whether any of the supplied data points lie outside of the expected pattern or dataset; these are called **outliers**. Being able to detect these sorts of anomalies can provide useful information to both your organization and as training material for your ML model.

Determining outliers has many applications, from intrusion detection to system health monitoring, and fraud detection in credit card transactions to fault detection in operating environments.

Anomalies fall broadly into three categories:

- **Point**: A single point of data is anomalous to the wider dataset
- **Contextual**: The anomaly is context specific
- **Collective**: A set of data points or collective direct to anomalous behaviors

Anomaly detection is similar to, but not the same as, noise removal.

Prediction

In the case of ML, prediction means using your dataset to make accurate guesses as to the likely outcome of or response to a relevant question based on already established (historical) data after training. Insights such as these provide tangible business value.

Sometimes, using the word *prediction* can be misleading. Oftentimes, you are not looking to forecast a future event, you're using ML to determine whether an event that has occurred is part of a valid dataset, or if it is anomalous, such as a fraud. In this case, you're making an educated guess as to the veracity of a data point—the event has already happened, you're just checking on its legitimacy.

Forecasting

The capacity to foresee the future would be an incredible superpower. However, with ML you can come fairly close. Being able to use a dataset based on a time series helps to further refine the model.

You use forecasting over time series to predict how time-dependent data might change in the future. This data can be, but is not limited to, the following:

- Daily, weekly, or monthly sales
- Changes to inventory
- Web traffic or capacity fluctuations
- Stock market price swings
- Sports results and betting odds

For managing data and predicting outcomes, companies, large and small, use a variety of techniques, ranging from basic spreadsheets to massive software applications. The whole point is to provide information to enable better decision making ability, by looking at historical data. These tools use this time series data to build forecast models to enable this.

This approach, though, is not without its downsides. Sometimes, forecast models find it difficult to make predictions in large datasets with irregular trends, or when combined datasets with independently changing variables change over time.

Clustering

A cluster refers to a collection of data points aggregated together because of similarities. There can be multiple clusters in a dataset—these types of dataset are most frequently analyzed using a K-means clustering algorithm.

K-means clustering is essentially a statistical technique where you're trying to determine a mean average (or center) of a cluster across a number (k) of clusters.

Feature or dimensionality reduction

This is a technique for reducing the number of dimensions that need to be analyzed, thereby reducing the complexity without necessarily reducing the amount of information that you are able to gather from the dataset.

Dimensions can be reduced by finding patterns between the dimensions: a co-variance.

There will be, by necessity, errors when performing a dimensionality reduction that need to be taken into account—the specifics of these errors will be due to the reduction algorithm used and the variance across the dataset as a whole.

Trees

Trees are used to model decisions in ML. Trees usually pose a question that has two (or more) possible responses—the simplest, two, is called a binary tree.

Trees are made up of branches and leaves. Branches are decision points and leaves are possible outcomes. The following diagram is an example of a decision tree:

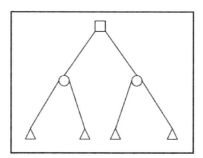

Classification

Classification is a technique for determining the class any dependent element belongs to based on one or more independent variables.

Classification data is used in the supervised learning branch of ML. It is used, initially, to train the model and then used to predict discrete independent system responses.

Interpolate missing data (sparsity)

If the data that you are collecting is sparse, in order to find meaningful and relevant information, you will need to interpolate to fill in the gaps. In data science, there is a technique called **L1 Norm Regularization** – this trains ML models (and AI) to look for patterns without *overfitting*.

Overfitting is a problem where an AI has been trained with a limited or sparse dataset, but it can match patterns and recognize elements in a more sophisticated way than its limited training allows for. When the AI sees something that it's not trained for (due to the limited training dataset), it can miscategorize. Using normalization or regularization techniques, AI can be trained to not overfit.

Image recognition

Images are a form of unstructured data, which means that ML (or DL) models and AI need to be specifically trained to identify and categorize them. For humans, sight, and therefore recognition of images, is vitally important; for training of AI, it is equally vitally important. Adding sight to an algorithm adds new capabilities.

AWS provides a service that manages images and video analysis and enables you to add this capability to your applications. Rekognition makes it easy to add this type of capability. You just provide an image or video to the Rekognition API, and the service can identify objects, people, text, scenes, and activities. It can also detect any inappropriate content. The service provides highly accurate facial analysis and facial recognition on visual content that you provide.

Pattern recognition

Analogous to image recognition is pattern recognition. Pattern recognition by ML and AI is generally through DL techniques, which attempt to replicate how human brains operate. DL does this by creating neural networks that can extract and understand complicated concepts and generate relationships from datasets.

Deep learning models are improved using complex pattern recognition of pictures, text, and sounds, which can help to create higher accuracy insights and predictions against incoming data.

Summary

In this chapter, we've covered a great detail of content. We've looked at several tools that will help you to build ML, DL, or AI models and we've looked at how to use Terraform to add them to your infrastructure. Where the tools are on the cutting edge of Terraform, we've noted that too.

You've also explored some of the concepts around machine learning, deep learning, and AI.

The content covered in this chapter, even though brief, provides a foundation to each of the topics and provides enough information to get started with integrating the tools into your infrastructure.

Next, you'll explore how to monitor your infrastructure and the applications that are housed there.

Exercises

Many ML and DL tools supplied by AWS are not covered by Terraform. Much of the effort that goes into making Terraform what it is comes in the form of open source contributions. Take a look into some of the projects around Terraform and see whether you can help out. Not only will you get satisfaction in helping, you will also get a better understanding of the Terraform sub-system.

Further reading

- **Anomaly detection**: https://www.datascience.com/blog/python-anomaly-detection
- **Caching**: https://aws.amazon.com/caching/
- **Prediction**: https://www.datarobot.com/wiki/prediction/

12
Observability - Understanding How Your Products Are Behaving

In this chapter, you will explore patterns for service management and customer experience. An overview of self-service options will be presented to allow product owners to investigate, diagnose, and resolve issues independently. Consolidating your event streams from your services and using the AWS dashboard to visualize your product performance and productivity will be the main highlights of this chapter. You'll understand service interactions and learn how to measure your customer experience. Finally, you'll be able to define service-level objectives for your product.

In brief, this chapter will cover the following topics:

- Logging
- Metrics
- Capacity management
- Tracing
- Alarms
- Events

Technical requirements

For this chapter, if you want to try things out, you will need to have the AWS CLI installed alongside Terraform (see https://aws.amazon.com/cli/ for instructions on how to install this on your system). Most of the functionality in this chapter will be in the form of CLI requests. This is because, once the initial Terraform set up is done for these AWS products, the remaining interactions can only be done through AWS Management Console or the CLI tool.

Analyzing your products

There's no point in running an environment and having products out in the wild if you don't understand how they are behaving; you can't just assume everything is fine. In fact, you need to work from the standpoint that nothing is fine and that it can all break at any time.

When you look at your environment in this manner, you will begin to realize that you need data in order to figure out what the issues are and how you might be able to resolve them. In theory, you will need to observe everything. The downside to all of this is that you will end up with a surplus of data—and, as a result, you will probably be swamped. In practice, however, observing everything (that is, every possible aspect of all of the tools in play) is impractical. You will need to decide what to watch in order to receive the best possible amount of information to be alerted to, find, and understand where an issue has developed.

We will start with logging.

Logging

Logging refers to the collection of data that describes what a system is doing at any one point in time. There are several different types of logs that are used to understand the state of a system over time: error (or exception) logs, heartbeat logs, and status logs. Different types of servers may also create other types of logs—for instance, Apache HTTPd creates an access log to keep track of request URLs that have been accessed.

Error or exception logs are collected when a system is in the act of doing something that is either unexpected or exceptional to its normal operating conditions. Status logs just collect data on the system status periodically. Heartbeat logs are set up to determine whether a system is active; something *pings* the application at set intervals for a health check.

All of these log types have something in common. They all collect data over time, which can be analyzed when necessary to determine how, why, and when a system state has been reached—this is usually if there is an issue with the system.

If your system logs to static log files, you will need to provide a rotation mechanism as these files have a tendency to get very large (that is, multi-gigabyte large) fairly quickly, so daily rotation might be an option.

In AWS, static log files are generally not an option and there is a better choice: CloudWatch. CloudWatch is the standard tool in the AWS ecosystem that provides logging, metric analysis, and alarm functionality.

You'll discover metrics data collection and analysis, and alarms in the following sections.

Metrics

Metrics are the measured elements in data, which are collected in the logs. Metrics form the basis of any information that can be obtained from the system for the purposes of analyzation and presentation.

The following sections first discuss the tool, CloudWatch, and then alarms.

CloudWatch

By default, several services provide free metrics for resources (such as Amazon EC2 instances, Amazon EBS volumes, and Amazon RDS DB instances). You can also enable detailed monitoring for some resources, such as your Amazon EC2 instances, or publish your own application metrics. Amazon CloudWatch can load all of the metrics in your account (both AWS resource metrics and the application metrics that you provide) to enable facilities around search; for visualizing the data, for example, in the AWS CloudWatch dashboard; and by providing configurable alarms, such as monitoring usage thresholds, CPU utilization, and more.

The next sections will cover how to create and maintain your alarms. Unfortunately, due to some limitations in Terraform, you can only create alarm resources. Other maintenance tasks are performed using the command console or the CLI.

As a quick primer, to create alarms in CloudWatch, you will need to add them to a namespace. Namespaces should really be logical units that mirror the responsibilities of your environment. This makes the alarms easier to find and maintain, their issues easier to keep track of, and the dashboards more pertinent to the information that they are being used to display.

The following subsections will discuss alarm creation and management.

Creating metric alarms

The following example shows how to create a metric alarm; this particular alarm is namespaced to `AWS/EC2` and triggers when the CPU utilization hits a threshold of an average of 80% over two evaluation periods of 120 seconds:

```
resource "aws_cloudwatch_metric_alarm" "foobar" {
  alarm_name = "terraform-test-foobar5"
  comparison_operator = "GreaterThanOrEqualToThreshold"
  evaluation_periods = "2"
  metric_name = "CPUUtilization"
  namespace = "AWS/EC2"
  period = "120"
  statistic = "Average"
  threshold = "80"
  alarm_description = "This metric monitors ec2 cpu utilization"
  insufficient_data_actions = []
}
```

Alarms can take many options (far too many to cover here); if you're interested in finding out more, then you can view the options in the Terraform documentation, which is available at https://www.terraform.io/docs/providers/aws/r/cloudwatch_metric_alarm.html.

We'll use the CLI or management console to explore the various options that are available to you in the following sections.

Viewing available metrics

As we've already covered namespaces, we'll dive straight into exploring how to view the available metrics using the CLI.

On your Terminal, type the following command:

```
$ aws cloudwatch list-metrics --namespace AWS/EC2
```

This command will return a JSON object, keyed on `"Metrics"`:

```
{
   "Metrics" : [
      {
         "Namespace": "AWS/EC2",
         "Dimensions": [
            {
               "Name": "InstanceId",
               "Value": "i-1234567890abcdef0"
            }
         ],
         "MetricName": "NetworkOut"
      }
   ]
}
```

> You can find more information at `https://docs.aws.amazon.com/AmazonCloudWatch/latest/monitoring/viewing_metrics_with_cloudwatch.html`.

Searching for available metrics

Searching for available metrics can only be done through the management console.

First, navigate to `https://console.aws.amazon.com/cloudwatch/`; then, select **Metrics** from the navigation pane and enter the search term that you require in the search field under the **All Metrics** tab—this returns the namespaces that are associated with the search term.

> You can find more information at `https://docs.aws.amazon.com/AmazonCloudWatch/latest/monitoring/finding_metrics_with_cloudwatch.html`.

Getting statistics for a metric

Statics for metrics can be obtained in a number of different ways depending on what information you need.

Getting the statistics for a single metric is achieved by using the following CLI command:

```
aws cloudwatch get-metric-statistics --namespace AWS/EC2 --metric-name <MetricName> \
--dimensions Name=InstanceId,Value=<MetricID> --statistics Maximum \
--start-time <Start DateTime> --end-time <End DateTime> --period 360
```

This will return a JSON object that holds two keys: `"Datapoints"` and `"Label"`. The `"Datapoints"` element is an array of data point objects that detail the value, value type, and date and time:

```
{
    "Datapoints": [
        {
            "Timestamp": "2016-10-19T00:18:00Z",
            "Maximum": 0.33000000000000002,
            "Unit": "Percent"
        },
        {
            "Timestamp": "2016-10-19T03:18:00Z",
            "Maximum": 99.670000000000002,
            "Unit": "Percent"
        },
        {
            "Timestamp": "2016-10-19T07:18:00Z",
            "Maximum": 0.34000000000000002,
            "Unit": "Percent"
        },
        ...
    ],
    "Label": "CPUUtilization"
}
```

You may find that you want aggregated data for a particular metric instead—this can be over resources, autoscaling groups, or **Amazon Machine Images** (**AMIs**). One thing to bear in mind is that CloudWatch is not able to aggregate data across regions because they are segregated.

In order to do this with the CLI, you could use something that is similar to the following commands:

```
aws cloudwatch get-metric-statistics --namespace AWS/EC2 --metric-name <MetricName> --statistics <AggregationFunction> "SampleCount" --start-time <Start DateTime> --end-time <End DateTime> --period 3600

aws cloudwatch get-metric-statistics --namespace AWS/EC2 --metric-name <MetricName>
```

```
--dimensions Name=AutoScalingGroupName,Value=<Value> --statistics
<AggregationFunction> "SampleCount" \
--start-time <Start DateTime> --end-time <End DateTime> --period 360

aws cloudwatch get-metric-statistics --namespace AWS/EC2 --metric-name
<MetricName> \
--dimensions Name=ImageId,Value=<AMIID> --statistics <AggregrationFunction>
\
--start-time <Start DateTime> --end-time <End DateTime> --period 3600
```

This will return data that is similar to the previous example response, but with a different data point object, respectively, as follows:

```
{
    "SampleCount": 238.0,
    "Timestamp": "2016-10-12T07:18:00Z",
    "Average": 0.038235294117647062,
    "Unit": "Percent"
}

{
    "SampleCount": 18.0,
    "Timestamp": "2016-10-19T21:36:00Z",
    "Sum": 0.0,
    "Unit": "Bytes"
}

{
    "Timestamp": "2016-10-10T07:00:00Z",
    "Average": 0.041000000000000009,
    "Unit": "Percent"
}
```

Here, the response returns the number of data points used in the sample and the aggregated result.

All of these work off the `get-metric-statistics` CLI function; more details can be found at https://docs.aws.amazon.com/cli/latest/reference/cloudwatch/get-metric-statistics.html.

Graphing metrics

Creating graphs of metrics is achieved using AWS Management Console.

Observability - Understanding How Your Products Are Behaving

In order to create a graph, you need to log in to `https://console.aws.amazon.com/cloudwatch/`. From there you can use the **All Metrics** tab to find and select the metric(s) that you want to create a chart for.

Once these selections have been made, you can provide additional metadata for the horizontal axis in order to help to present your data.

Once the chart is set up correctly, you can share a URL or add it to a dashboard.

Editing a chart is pretty much the same, however, created charts are found under the **Graphed Metrics** tab.

Publishing custom metrics

You can use the CLI or an API to publish your own custom metrics. With the management console, you can view the output of these custom metrics in visual form—graphs.

There are several ways of setting up these kinds of metrics:

- **High-resolution metrics**: These metrics are those that have a granularity of one second; standard-resolution metrics (the default) have a one minute granularity. High-resolution metrics give a more immediate insight into the your application's activity, but this leads to higher charges as the `PutMetricData` call is charged.
- **Dimensions**: Using the `--dimensions` argument is common in custom metric definition. Each metric can have up to 10 dimensions. Dimensions are defined using a key-value pair. Different creation commands use different definition formats; for instance, the `put-metric data uses a Key=Value` format:

    ```
    aws cloudwatch put-metric-data --metric-name Buffers --namespace
    MyNameSpace --unit Bytes --value 231434333 --dimensions
    InstanceId=1-23456789,InstanceType=m1.small
    ```

    `get-metric-statistics` uses a `Name=name,Value=value` format, as shown in the following command:

    ```
    aws cloudwatch get-metric-statistics --metric-name Buffers --
    namespace MyNameSpace --dimensions Name=InstanceId,Value=1-23456789
    Name=InstanceType,Value=m1.small --start-time 2016-10-15T04:00:00Z
    --end-time 2016-10-19T07:00:00Z --statistics Average --period 60
    ```

- **Single data points**: To publish a single data point for a new or existing metric, use the `put-metric-data` command with one value and a timestamp:

    ```
    aws cloudwatch put-metric-data --metric-name PageViewCount --namespace MyService --value 2 --timestamp 2016-10-20T12:00:00.000Z
    aws cloudwatch put-metric-data --metric-name PageViewCount --namespace MyService --value 4 --timestamp 2016-10-20T12:00:01.000Z
    aws cloudwatch put-metric-data --metric-name PageViewCount --namespace MyService --value 5 --timestamp 2016-10-20T12:00:02.000Z
    ```

- **Publishing statistic sets**: Data can be aggregated before publishing to CloudWatch. Aggregration minimizes the number of calls to `put-metric-data` (hence reducing the amount of charge):

    ```
    aws cloudwatch put-metric-data --metric-name PageViewCount --namespace MyService --statistic-values Sum=11,Minimum=2,Maximum=5,SampleCount=3 --timestamp 2016-10-14T12:00:00.000Z
    ```

- **Publish the value zero**: If the data that you're collecting is sparse, you may require to publish zero rather than no value. You can use this for setting CloudWatch alarms.

> You can find out more information at https://docs.aws.amazon.com/AmazonCloudWatch/latest/monitoring/publishingMetrics.html.

Using metric math

Metric math is used to query multiple CloudWatch metrics and uses them to create a new time series based on that data. The new time series can be visualized in the CloudWatch console. These operations can also be created using the `GetMetricData` API.

The amount of functionality that can be created using the `GetMetricData` API is too large to be covered here (for more details see https://docs.aws.amazon.com/AmazonCloudWatch/latest/monitoring/using-metric-math.html).

Now that you understand how to find and view the information about your infrastructure and the applications that run on it, it's time to learn how to improve the performance to ensure that you're getting the best out of it. This is the subject of the next section.

Performance optimization

Being able to see the information about your system is the first step in fixing any issues that exist within it. With this data, you can create charted metrics to monitor your infrastructure for performance issues, and determine whether there are any hot spots, wait states (over- or under-utilization), or low utilization.

Armed with this information, you can alter your infrastructure to cater for these identified states.

However, as important as all of this is, much of this is time-consuming; first, you need to identify the data that provides the correct information, create all of the visualizations that you need; analyze and understand all of that data, make changes, and then rinse and repeat. AWS provides a tool that can help with all of this: AWS Trusted Advisor.

Trusted Advisor analyzes your infrastructure and any applications running on it and returns information on how to change your provisioning and configuration settings to ensure that AWS best practices are followed.

Capacity management

In many cases, the tools provided by AWS are managed services. This means that you don't need to worry about managing the capacity of the infrastructure that you're using.

For those parts of your system that are not managed services, the previously mentioned tools—CloudWatch and Trusted Advisor—can help.

Once you understand your utilization of these services, you can scale your EC2's and ECB's accordingly.

AWS dashboards

The AWS dashboards are user configurable elements of the CloudWatch console. You can use them to monitor your infrastructure on a single page even if those resources are spread across several regions.

The following sections cover the creation and management of dashboards.

Creating a dashboard

Creating a dashboard is a case of creating a name and populating the body, as follows:

```
resource "aws_cloudwatch_dashboard" "main" {
  dashboard_name = "my-dashboard"

  dashboard_body = <<EOF
{
  "widgets": [
     {
        "type":"metric",
        "x":0,
        "y":0,
        "width":12,
        "height":6,
        "properties":{
           "metrics":[
              [
                 "AWS/EC2",
                 "CPUUtilization",
                 "InstanceId",
                 "i-012345"
              ]
           ],
           "period":300,
           "stat":"Average",
           "region":"us-east-1",
           "title":"EC2 Instance CPU"
        }
     },
     {
        "type":"text",
        "x":0,
        "y":7,
        "width":3,
        "height":3,
        "properties":{
           "markdown":"Hello world"
        }
     }
  ]
}
EOF
}
```

The type of widgets available and number of elements that placed on a page can be found at https://docs.aws.amazon.com/AmazonCloudWatch/latest/APIReference/CloudWatch-Dashboard-Body-Structure.html.

Adding or removing a graph

To add a graph, you can log in to the CloudWatch console (https://console.aws.amazon.com/cloudwatch/), select **Dashboards** from the navigation panel, and then **Add widget**. Once there, you just need to follow the options to obtain and place the graph that you need in order to visualize the data.

To remove a graph, you can log in to the CloudWatch console (https://console.aws.amazon.com/cloudwatch/), select **Dashboards** from the navigation panel, and select the dashboard that you wish to remove. Then, hover over the title of the graph that you want to delete and select the **Delete** option.

Moving or resizing a graph

In order to move a graph, log in to the CloudWatch console (https://console.aws.amazon.com/cloudwatch/), select **Dashboards** from the navigation panel, and select the dashboard that you wish to edit. Then, hover over the title of the graph that you want to move until the selection icon appears, and then drag it into the new position.

In order to resize a graph, log in to the CloudWatch console (https://console.aws.amazon.com/cloudwatch/), select **Dashboards** from the navigation panel, and select the dashboard that you wish to edit. Then, hover over the graph and drag the bottom-right-hand corner of the graph to the required size.

Editing a graph

In order to edit a graph, you can log in to the CloudWatch console (https://console.aws.amazon.com/cloudwatch/), select **Dashboards** from the navigation panel, and then select the dashboard that you wish to edit.

From there, you can manipulate all of the elements that make up a graph.

Graphing metrics manually on a CloudWatch dashboard

Metrics are only selectable from the dashboard if the data has been published within 14 days. To add metrics with data that was published after this cut-off point, then you will need to manually update the graph configuration.

In order to edit a graph, you can log in to the CloudWatch console (https://console.aws.amazon.com/cloudwatch/), select **Dashboards** from the navigation panel, and then select the dashboard that you wish to edit.

With that selected, follow the **Actions** | **View/edit source** link. This will open up the editing window in order to see the underlying JSON configuration.

In the following example, add the expected metrics at the point marked in the structure:

```
{
    "type": "metric",
    "x": 0,
    "y": 0,
    "width": 6,
    "height": 3,
    "properties": {
        "view": "singleValue",
        "metrics": [
            [ "AWS/EBS", "VolumeReadOps", "VolumeId",
"vol-1234567890abcdef0" ],
            <<-- ADD METRICS HERE -->>
        ],
        "region": "us-west-1"
    }
},
```

The structure will be slightly different for your graph; all you need to remember is to update the "metrics" array with the metadata that you need to specify the extra metric.

Adding or removing a text widget

In order to move a graph, you can log in to the CloudWatch console (https://console.aws.amazon.com/cloudwatch/), select **Dashboards** from the navigation panel, and then select the dashboard that you wish to edit.

In order to add a widget, select **Add widget**, and then **Configure text**. Then, choose **Create** and **Save dashboard**.

In order to edit a widget, hover over the required widget, and then select **Widget actions** | **Edit**. Make the changes and **Update widget**; finally, select **Save dashboard**.

In order to remove a widget, hover over the required widget. Then, select **Widget actions** | **Delete** and, finally, select **Save dashboard**.

Adding or removing an alarm

In order to add an alarm, you can log in to the CloudWatch console (https://console.aws.amazon.com/cloudwatch/), select **Alarms** from the navigation panel and then **Add to dashboard**. Once there, you just need to follow the options to obtain and place the alarm that you need on the dashboard.

In order to remove a alarm, you can log in to the CloudWatch console (https://console.aws.amazon.com/cloudwatch/), select **Dashboards** from the navigation panel, and then select the dashboard that you wish to remove. Hover over the title of the graph that you want to delete and then select the **Delete** option.

Monitoring resources in multiple regions

In order to add a graph, you can log in to the CloudWatch console (https://console.aws.amazon.com/cloudwatch/) and select **Metrics** from the navigation panel. You can select the **Region** that you want from the navigation bar, and then you can select the metrics that you want to add to the dashboard. Once you've created the metric that you want data for, click on **Save Dashboard**.

Linking and unlinking graphs

In order to link graphs, you can log in to the CloudWatch console (https://console.aws.amazon.com/cloudwatch/), select **Dashboards** from the navigation panel, and then select the dashboard that you wish to edit. Then, select or unselect the **Actions | Link graphs** option.

Adding a dashboard to your favorites list

In order to mark a dashboard as a favorite, log in to the CloudWatch console (https://console.aws.amazon.com/cloudwatch/), select **Dashboards** from the navigation panel, and then select the star icon against the dashboard that you wish to mark as a favorite.

Changing the time range or time zone format

In order to change the time range or time zone format, log in to the CloudWatch console (https://console.aws.amazon.com/cloudwatch/), select **Dashboards** from the navigation panel, and then select the dashboard that you wish to edit. You can update the time range to one of the preoffered time ranges or select the **Custom** option. Once your changes are complete, click on **Save dashboard**.

Tracing

Tracing is the act of following the flow of data (such as requests and responses) through your system (the infrastructure and application) in order to provide information on how the system is functioning. This is usually performed when the system is doing something unexpected and you need to find out why.

Tracing in AWS is performed using X-Ray.

X-Ray

X-Ray is used to trace user requests through a system—these systems are usually, but not restricted to, those that are architected using modern techniques, such as RESTful API driven, **start of authority** (**SOA**), or microservices. It is used to trace these requests through the entire application stack and aggregates the findings in order to give an end-to-end overview of the application performance.

There are some limitations with X-Ray, however: only applications written in Java, Node.js (JavaScript), and .NET are supported along with EC2, Lambda, and Elastic Beanstalk services. However, even with these limitations, X-Ray can be helpful in finding performance bottlenecks, mapping connections and relationships between your application services and AWS services, and discovering where latencies occur across the infrastructure.

The complexity of the applications is totally transparent to X-Ray, as is the environment in which it is being executed; it works in both development and production environments. Applications can be simple, single client-server applications or n-tier applications (including web applications or multiservice microservices). They can also span regions, availability zones, and accounts.

X-Ray should be the first port of call if your application stack is misbehaving.

Alarms

Alarms are used to flag issues and exceptional circumstances when they arise. Alarm creation and maintenance has been covered earlier in this chapter in the *AWS dashboards* section.

In general, alarms are raised to cover the following circumstances:

- Fatigue
- When a large amount of error budget is being consumed
- Anomaly detection
- Thresholds

Amazon CloudWatch employs Amazon **Simple Notification Service (SNS)** to send emails, messages, or push notifications on mobile. The first step is to create and subscribe to an SNS topic. When a CloudWatch alarm is created, you can add the SNS topic to send an email notification when the alarm state changes.

Alarm states

An alarm has the following possible states:

- **OK**: In this state, the metric (or expression) is not beyond the defined threshold.
- **ALARM**: In this state, the metric or expression is beyond the defined threshold.
- **INSUFFICIENT_DATA**: In this state, there are three possible scenarios—the alarm has just started, the metric is unavailable, or sufficient data is not available for the metric to realize the alarm state.

The **period** is the duration required for evaluating the metric or expression so as to create every single data point for an alarm. It is usually expressed in seconds; however, if you choose one minute as the period, a data point will be generated every minute.

The **Evaluation Period** is the number of most recent periods (or data points) for evaluation when an alarm state is determined.

For more information on Amazon CloudWatch alarms, you can refer to the following website: `https://docs.aws.amazon.com/AmazonCloudWatch/latest/monitoring/AlarmThatSendsEmail.html`.

Datapoints to Alarm refers to the number of data points within the Evaluation Period that must be breached for the alarm to move to the ALARM state. The breaching data points don't need to be consecutive; rather, they should all just be within the last number of data points equal to the Evaluation Period.

A CloudWatch can be specified for each alarm to treat the missing data points in any of the following ways:

- `missing`: The alarm will disregard the missing data points while evaluating whether to change the state.
- `notBreaching`: The missing data points will be treated as within the threshold.
- `breaching`: The missing data points will be treated as beyond or breaching the threshold.
- `ignore`: The current alarm state will be maintained.

How the alarm state is evaluated when data is missing

Irrespective of the value being set for treating missing data, the moment that an alarm evaluates whether the state should be changed, CloudWatch will attempt to retrieve data points that are much higher in number than those identified by the Evaluation Periods. The precise data points that CloudWatch will try to retrieve will depend on the period length of the alarm and whether (on the basis of this) it has a standard or high resolution. The evaluation range is the data point time frame that CloudWatch attempts for retrieval.

After the retrieval of the data points, the following happens:

- If all of the data points are present within the evaluation range, then CloudWatch will evaluate the alarm based on the data points that are newest.
- If a few data points are missing from the evaluation range, but the number of existing data points that have been retrieved is equal to or more than the alarm's Evaluation Periods, then the evaluation of the alarm state will be on the basis of the newest data points that were retrieved successfully. Here, the value set for treating missing data is of no value and will have to be ignored.
- If a few data points are missing from the evaluation range, and the existing data points that are retrieved are lower than the number of Evaluation Periods for the alarm, then CloudWatch will plug in the gap with the missing data points. This will be done with the results that have been specified on how to treat absent data. Then, it will proceed toward evaluating the alarm. That said, any actual data points within this particular evaluation range, irrespective of when they were reported, will be evaluated. CloudWatch will use the absent data points as sparingly as possible.

In all of these situations, the number of data points evaluated will always be equal to the value of the Evaluation Periods. If fewer than the value of Datapoints to Alarm are breaching, then the alarm state will be set to OK; otherwise, the state will be set to ALARM.

With that now under your belt, you'll look at events and how to set up logging them in CloudWatch.

Events

Events are messages in response to an action. The action can be anything from user interactions with your application to intra-service messages. They can come from internal and external sources.

CloudWatch events are system events that are logged in near real time in order to describe changes in the infrastructure. Simple rules are used to map events to streams for analysis.

Concepts

Before you begin using CloudWatch Events, you should understand the following concepts:

- **Events**: A change in the AWS environment is indicated by an event. Events can be generated by AWS sources when their state undergoes any changes. AWS CloudTrail publishes events when an API call is made. Custom application-level events can be generated and published to CloudWatch Events. We can also set up scheduled events on a periodic basis. For a list of services that generate events, and sample events from each service, you can refer to *CloudWatch Events Event Examples From Supported Services* (https://docs.aws.amazon.com/AmazonCloudWatch/latest/events/EventTypes.html).
- **Targets**: A target processes events and receives events in JSON format. The following AWS services can be used as targets:
    - Amazon EC2 instances
    - AWS Lambda functions
    - Streams in Amazon Kinesis Data Streams
    - Delivery streams in Amazon Kinesis Data Firehose
    - Amazon ECS tasks
    - Systems Manager Run Command
    - Systems Manager Automation
    - AWS Batch jobs
    - Step Functions state machines
    - Pipelines in AWS CodePipeline
    - AWS CodeBuild projects

- Amazon Inspector assessment templates
- Amazon SNS topics
- Amazon SQS queues
- Built-in targets—such as the EC2 `CreateSnapshot` API call, the EC2 `RebootInstances` API call, the EC2 `StopInstances` API call, and the EC2 `TerminateInstances` API call
- The default event bus of another AWS account

- **Rules**: By definition, a rule matches incoming events and routes them to targets for processing. Multiple targets can be routed to through a single rule, and all of these targets will be processed in parallel. No particular order is maintained for processing rules; the advantage of this is that different parts of an organization can identify and process events that seem interesting. By passing only certain parts or overwriting with a constant, a rule can be used to customize a JSON that is sent to the target.

You can try sending a notification (Slack) or call an external endpoint (pagerduty) with your Lambda, as shown in the following code block:

```
resource "aws_cloudwatch_event_rule" "console" {
  name = "capture-aws-sign-in"
  description = "Capture each AWS Console Sign In"

  event_pattern = <<PATTERN
{
  "detail-type": [
    "AWS Console Sign In via CloudTrail"
  ]
}
PATTERN
}

resource "aws_cloudwatch_event_target" "sns" {
  rule = "${aws_cloudwatch_event_rule.console.name}"
  target_id = "SendToSNS"
  arn = "${aws_sns_topic.aws_logins.arn}"
}

resource "aws_cloudwatch_event_target" "ec2_target" {
  rule = "${aws_cloudwatch_event_rule.ec2_events.name}"
  arn = "${aws_lambda_function.eventwatch_lambda.arn}"
}

resource "aws_sns_topic" "aws_logins" {
  name = "aws-console-logins"
```

```
}

resource "aws_sns_topic_policy" "default" {
  arn = "${aws_sns_topic.aws_logins.arn}"
  policy = "${data.aws_iam_policy_document.sns_topic_policy.json}"
}

data "aws_iam_policy_document" "sns_topic_policy" {
  statement {
    effect = "Allow"
    actions = ["SNS:Publish"]

    principals {
      type = "Service"
      identifiers = ["events.amazonaws.com"]
    }

    resources = ["${aws_sns_topic.aws_logins.arn}"]
  }
}
```

Add events with `put-events` (https://docs.aws.amazon.com/cli/latest/reference/events/put-events.html) for testing.

Summary

In this chapter, we covered how to observe your application with logging, metrics, and tracing. We also looked at events and how to track them. When set up, all of this will help you to track changes in your infrastructure, find inconsistencies, and provide insights in order to process improvements. In the next chapter, we will analyze persistence paradigms that are ineffective and may result in undesired consequences.

Exercises

- Set up a dashboard that holds some graphs that monitor your infrastructure.
- Use X-Ray to map out the system interactions. Then, use this as a baseline for when there is an issue with your infrastructure.

Further reading

- To learn more about monitoring services not covered in this chapter, check out the video masterclass on monitoring with AWS CloudWatch at `https://prod.packtpub.com/in/networking-and-servers/aws-masterclass-monitoring-and-devops-aws-cloudwatch-video`.
- Further details on creating and maintaining graphs of metrics can be found at `https://docs.aws.amazon.com/AmazonCloudWatch/latest/monitoring/graph_metrics.html`.
- For more information in maintaining dashboards, you can visit `https://docs.aws.amazon.com/AmazonCloudWatch/latest/monitoring/CloudWatch_Dashboards.html`.
- For in depth monitoring practices for your applications see *Hands-On Microservices - Monitoring and Testing* at `https://prod.packtpub.com/in/application-development/hands-on-microservices-monitoring-and-testing`.
- Visualizing your log data with Kibana is discussed in depth in this book: `https://prod.packtpub.com/in/big-data-and-business-intelligence/kibana-7-quick-start-guide`.
- The golden signals originated from Google; their original publication is available at `https://landing.google.com/sre/sre-book/chapters/monitoring-distributed-systems/`.

13
Anti-Patterns - Bypassing Inferior Options

Most data anti-patterns are schema design-and application-focused and so are out of the scope of this book. By identifying bottlenecks in data persistence, retrieval, and storage, we find anti-patterns that can be addressed programmatically. We encourage you to review processes within your organization to break out of consequences related to Conway's law (as a quick reminder: systems mirror the communication structures of the organization that designed them).

It is imperative that you try to remain flexible in your solutions—try to use the right tool for the job. In some cases, it's not all that clear cut which tool is the right one as there may be several options; this is where experimentation comes in.

The design of the system should maximize the portability of your data. One way is by adhering to established standards and reducing the amount of vendor lock-in that you have in your system. This will ensure that new technologies can be easily adopted without complicated transformations by program code or long laborious data migration programs.

As an aside to all of this, the less non-business related code (infrastructure, scaffolding, and so on) that exists in and around a system, the less data transformation and data verification debugging needs to take place. Debugging unexpected changes to data, schemas, and meta data can be quite difficult and time-consuming.

The following topics will be covered in brief in this chapter:

- Building processes
- Best practices
- Different patterns

Building processes

The data world is slowly moving toward agile development life cycles that improve feedback time, which in turn improves experiment frequency and data quality.

Time-consuming upfront design, read *waterfall*, has been found to not necessarily correlate with increased return on investment. Designing the data structures upfront means that you're likely to miss out on opportunities that you can find by experimentation. Upfront design signals that your organization is most likely unwilling to explore newer technologies and handle some of the risk that accompanies them, and therefore, it can fail to grow. This philosophy of *tried and tested* runs, in part, counter to being on AWS and everything that it has to offer.

Having some idea of the kind of data that you might need helps to move toward agile development practices, which in turn reduces the requirement to fully design data structures/schemas upfront, making them iterative changes, as more elements/requirements of the application build become apparent.

Additionally, many development frameworks provide the ability to generate database and data changes alongside code changes, so that they are aligned and can be changed in concert with each other. In practice, database changes become code changes that are then stored in version control, so a record is available of the growth of the database. Database changes are then handled the same as code changes on application deployment, using CI tools with little need for separate, manual intervention by multiple teams in a convoluted, error-prone deployment strategy.

Ultimately, the aim is to not be dependent on other teams to deploy your product. Having data structures managed as code helps gain that autonomy.

When you look at the types of storage that are available to you, the increased storage density, in conjunction with continued decreases in costs, provide further impetus for *keeping everything*.

Keeping everything has several benefits that might be more important to the business that you work for over and above the cost. Having access to a large pool of data provides mining opportunities for information that hasn't been thought about in the initial design, provides adherence to various regions' data protection frameworks, and, if sufficiently anonymized, can be used to provide test data for application iterations.

All of this means that processes can be developed to manage and improve the quality of your data, and also improve the shape and flow of data through your environment.

Analysis paralysis

We're not going to have perfect information, but we need to get moving:

> *Analysis paralysis occurs when the team, or more often the data professionals on the team, discover that it's incredibly difficult and time-consuming to get people to agree to the one truth about their data.*
>
> *– Scott Ambler* (http://agiledata.org/essays/oneTruth.html)

Pick a solution and move forward; we can't always get things right the first time and neither should we expect to. One motto to follow is *build fast, fail early*. This means that your team (or your organization) should accept, or maybe even actively seek out, failures and treat them as learning opportunities. It's easy to change things when your application is small and under active development, but its rather a different thing to re-architect the underlying data structures in a production-released application.

Favor small incremental cycles that build on each other; this way you can measure improvements and gauge early in the process if you need to change anything. Again, we can't stress highly enough, making changes early in the development process is far easier and less expensive than if these things become tech debt or end up being toxic elements left in the build to be dealt with later on in the project life cycle (or in some cases never) when they are much more difficult and costly to change.

In the main, big architectural efforts upfront lead to lost opportunities and usually waste money. These efforts usually spring from being unwilling to explore newer alternatives to those that are *tried and tested*. Without having the space or the willingness to experiment, organizations are not able to grasp at technologies that might give them the edge on their competitors.

Trash

Do not throw away your data if you can possibly help it; this may seem counterproductive and expensive though. Why keep a vast lake of data that takes up space and costs money. The point is that without this data, your organization doesn't have a reservoir of readily available data to mine for additional insights into its customer base, nor would it be possible for an organization to rebuild its live storage data/cache data should disaster strike. As a team (or organization), it needs to be understood that different types of data have their own life cycle needs, but AWS provides many good solutions for reducing long-term storage costs, for example S3 Glacier and the newer S3 Glacier Deep Archive.

Setting up a Glacier vault through Terraform is straightforward as shown in the following example:

```
resource "aws_sns_topic" "aws_sns_topic" {
  name = "glacier-sns-topic"
}

resource "aws_glacier_vault" "my_archive" {
  name = "MyArchive"
  notification {
    sns_topic = "${aws_sns_topic.aws_sns_topic.arn}"
    events = ["ArchiveRetrievalCompleted", "InventoryRetrievalCompleted"]
  }
  access_policy = <<EOF
{
    "Version":"2012-10-17",
    "Statement":[
      {
        "Sid": "add-read-only-perm",
        "Principal": "*",
        "Effect": "Allow",
        "Action": [
           "glacier:InitiateJob",
           "glacier:GetJobOutput"
        ],
        "Resource": "arn:aws:glacier:eu-west-1:432981146916:vaults/MyArchive"
      }
    ]
}
EOF
  tags = {
    Test = "MyArchive"
  }
}
```

To read more about Glacier, go to: https://aws.amazon.com/glacier/?nc2=h_m1. More specifics on how to set this up with Terraform can be found at https://www.terraform.io/docs/providers/aws/r/glacier_vault.html.

If you need to aggregate or summarize your information after its useful shelf life, do it out of band and provide it to your consumers—AWS provides services that can help with this.

Best practices

Avoid *one size fits all* solutions. One size doesn't usually fit all situations that you might need to cater for. Think about the various needs of your application/use cases and design accordingly some things to consider, such as document storage, relational storage, graph storage, caching, data stream processing, image processing, high availability, high consistency, distributed nodes, latency, transaction support. This list is not exhaustive.

Take time to fully understand the life cycle of your tools of choice and data that you are charged with caring for. This includes tool upgrade time frames and assessing compatibility issues after upgrade. High incidences of upgrades for a toolchain might be a consideration for discounting it for production services as there may be stability or compatibility issues between versions.

Where practical, find the bleeding edge for your toolchain and map your journey to it. It will pay dividends if you understand upcoming features so you can plan ahead and, therefore, take advantage of them. What you will need to watch out for is the hype cycle. Don't get caught up in chasing the latest features for your toolchain without assessing whether or not they are beneficial. That ultra-cool feature that you want to use in the latest patch could also be accompanied with other changes that cause data incompatibilities, which can make backing out of the change impossible.

The single most important takeaway from this section is to take small, measured risks through continuous experimentation.

Tight coupling

To this day, it is unavoidable that underlying data structures influence the design of any application that uses those structures, even after applying ORM, ODM, and other techniques.

Using database schema migration tools such as Flyway or Active Record empower your DBAs and developers to make incremental and mostly reversible changes; in general, frameworks call this process migration. These changes can be enforced and reviewed as a process prior to pushing them to a production server. There is also the additional benefit of being able to keep a basic audit trail of changes by enabling DBAs and developers to push these to version control. None of this is without danger, however. As with all things, poor, ill-advised, or irreversible changes can still get through, even when comprehensive test frameworks and human review procedures are used.

Treating your data in the same manner as any other service decouples it from the patch and upgrade cycles of your tooling. Whilst this does not give free rein to upgrade tooling at will, it does allow upgrades and patches to happen in a controlled manner, ensuring that data is protected.

Interface segregation (usually by API) provides a further mechanism for lowering friction between teams developing services independently. Each team should provide stubs or mock services that conform to the established API designs in order to allow for the interface segregation—others teams can build their own services against these provided mocks, making them independent of each other. These mock services are then useful for testing and integrations. Tools such as GraphQL can help with the design.

Because services will be built against provided APIs, designs will be coupled to that particular design, so it becomes incumbent on the development team to either communicate changes and/or versions of the API. Versioning is usually the better option, as it isolates customers from API changes, as long as the underlying data structure contains all the data required to power all the versions.

One further option here is to create nano and microservices. These small services can provide the necessary abstractions to the data.

Lock-in

The bleeding edge is a fun place to be. You can't live there forever. Don't stay there forever.

Rapid changes in a service's API and slow application feature development may put your product in jeopardy. Lack of support, community, or paid for and a dearth of trained specialists can derail your product adoption as you scale.

Amazon's commitment to a variety of stable and well-known open source projects allows you to prototype quickly and evolve steadily. The AWS catalog, in conjunction with marketplace offerings and container support, provides you with many alternatives for data services.

Being in a vendor lock-in situation, while this might be seen as preferable from a business or expenditure point of view initially, can create a growing number of problems as the contracts are allowed to span a significant, increased expense; difficult data extraction; reduced support over time; no or limited upgrade path; deprecation of business critical services, and end of life issues.

These problems should be drivers away from products and services that have vendor lock-ins, as they make the process of migration much more difficult, risky, and costly.

Businesses might find these costs unpalatable if some or all of the business critical systems are locked-in in this way.

Everything is a nail

Once you get comfortable with a toolset, it is hard to see the limitations of what it can provide and it's difficult to understand the benefits of looking outside of a known toolset to those without prior knowledge and experience in other paradigms.

As an example, traditional SQL databases have been around for a long time and can handle very large datasets quite easily, alongside which they have an accessible syntax. Talent is readily available for hire. TensorFlow or Elasticsearch may be things that provide the functionality that is required to achieve the final aims of the project, or maybe just migrating from SQL to DynamoDB covers it. You will, however, need to take into account any learning curves, or the cost of hiring new engineers with the relevant skillsets, before moving toward new technologies, especially if they are vastly different from the in-house toolset.

Think about what questions you need to answer today to get to your next project milestone. It might be feasible to begin the work on a project using one type of datastore to hit a particular milestone and then migrate to another for the next.

There is a case for taking the hit on newer, lesser known technologies if they help you achieve your goal, but don't jump on the bandwagon of the newest, coolest tech on the market, just because it's cool. It has to be necessary to the successful completion of your project, otherwise it just becomes an unnecessary cost and time sink.

All of these decisions are subjective and dependent on the appetite for change in your organization—if you're in the process of migrating, there might a great appetite for change; temper this with pragmatism and use only what you need. Again, be wary of just plain substitution of old for old on AWS.

Different patterns

As your data volume grows, migrate toward toolsets that can handle your transformation and storage needs. To put it colorfully, avoid the bazooka, if all you need is a bow and arrow—there are others that could be used here hammer/nails for example. Continue to invest in new technologies where necessary, while ensuring that day-to-day business needs are kept stable, patched, and running.

Polyglot persistence

Taking advantage of the right technology for your persistence needs limits your exposure to unnecessary maintenance challenges. Microservice architectures give you the opportunity to choose the appropriate data structure for your business needs. When choosing a provider, factor in the learning and development costs, as well as the maintenance costs of your choice.

Technical debt often makes sense while rushing to get your product to market. As you pivot to meet your customers needs, data models can change rapidly. An unstructured notation may give you greater flexibility in the short term. A mature product may demand a platform capable of handling larger volumes of more structured information—this may mean converting from an unstructured design to a structured data schema. In any case, keeping response times reasonable will be critical to the survival of your product.

The design of your system might need to make use of many different types of persistence. You might need a search index, a message queue, document storage, key-value storage, caches or relational data storage, or you might just need to search over the data that you have in S3 in a serverless manner. For each of these, AWS has at least one solution.

The following sections show how to set some of these up.

Athena

For serverless queries over data in S3, use Athena, which can be used in the following manner:

```
resource "aws_s3_bucket" "hoge" {
  bucket = "tf-test"
}

resource "aws_athena_database" "hoge" {
  name = "users"
  bucket = "${aws_s3_bucket.hoge.bucket}"
}

resource "aws_athena_named_query" "foo" {
  name = "bar"
  database = "${aws_athena_database.hoge.name}"
  query = "SELECT * FROM ${aws_athena_database.hoge.name} limit 10;"
}
```

Amazon Simple Queue Service (SQS)

AWS provides several different queue types, this being one, as the name suggests :

```
resource "aws_sqs_queue" "terraform_queue" {
  name = "terraform-example-queue"
  delay_seconds = 90
  max_message_size = 2048
  message_retention_seconds = 86400
  receive_wait_time_seconds = 10
  redrive_policy = "{\"deadLetterTargetArn\":\"${aws_sqs_queue.terraform_queue_deadletter.arn}\",\"maxReceiveCount\":4}"

  tags = {
    Environment = "production"
  }
}
```

DocumentDB

DocumentDB, which has compatibility with MongoDB, is a schemaless document store. For all intents and purposes, if you are familiar with MongoDB, then DocumentDB will hold few surprises.

An example for setting up a cluster of DocumentDB is as follows:

```
resource "aws_docdb_cluster_instance" "cluster_instances" {
  count = 2
  identifier = "docdb-cluster-demo-${count.index}"
  cluster_identifier = "${aws_docdb_cluster.default.id}"
  instance_class = "db.r4.large"
}

resource "aws_docdb_cluster" "default" {
  cluster_identifier = "docdb-cluster-demo"
  availability_zones = ["us-west-2a", "us-west-2b", "us-west-2c"]
  master_username = "foo"
  master_password = "barbut8chars"
}
```

DynamoDB

DynamoDB is both a key-value store and a document datastore. As it is serverless, to set it up, you just need to add a table definition as follows:

```
resource "aws_dynamodb_table" "basic-dynamodb-table" {
  name = "TableName"
  billing_mode = "PROVISIONED"
  read_capacity = 20
  write_capacity = 20
  hash_key = "UserId"
  range_key = "Id"

  attribute {
    name = "UserId"
    type = "S"
  }

  attribute {
    name = "Id"
    type = "S"
  }

  ttl {
    attribute_name = "TimeToExist"
    enabled = false
  }
}
```

ElastiCache

ElastiCache provides services to cater for different needs: Memcached and Redis. The following is an example of setting up a Redis cluster:

```
resource "aws_elasticache_cluster" "example" {
  cluster_id = "cluster-example"
  engine = "redis"
  node_type = "cache.m4.large"
  num_cache_nodes = 1
  parameter_group_name = "default.redis3.2"
  engine_version = "3.2.10"
  port = 6379
}
```

Redshift

Technically, Redshift is designed for data warehousing, but it has the ability to extend queries over the data lake, so I've added it here.

To set Redshift up, you will need a Redshift cluster and a service account linked to an S3 bucket as per the following two listings:

```
data "aws_redshift_cluster" "test_cluster" {
  cluster_identifier = "test-cluster"
}

resource "aws_kinesis_firehose_delivery_stream" "test_stream" {
  name = "terraform-kinesis-firehose-test-stream"
  destination = "redshift"

  s3_configuration {
    role_arn = "${aws_iam_role.firehose_role.arn}"
    bucket_arn = "${aws_s3_bucket.bucket.arn}"
    buffer_size = 10
    buffer_interval = 400
    compression_format = "GZIP"
  }

  redshift_configuration {
    role_arn = "${aws_iam_role.firehose_role.arn}"
    cluster_jdbcurl =
"jdbc:redshift://${data.aws_redshift_cluster.test_cluster.endpoint}/${data.aws_redshift_cluster.test_cluster.database_name}"
    username = "testuser"
    password = "T3stPass"
    data_table_name = "test-table"
    copy_options = "delimiter '|'" # the default delimiter
    data_table_columns = "test-col"
  }
}

data "aws_redshift_service_account" "main" {}

resource "aws_s3_bucket" "bucket" {
  bucket = "tf-redshift-logging-test-bucket"
  force_destroy = true

  policy = <<EOF
{
    "Version": "2008-10-17",
    "Statement": [
        {
```

```
                    "Sid": "Put bucket policy needed for audit logging",
                    "Effect": "Allow",
                    "Principal": {
                        "AWS": "${data.aws_redshift_service_account.main.arn}"
                    },
                    "Action": "s3:PutObject",
                    "Resource": "arn:aws:s3:::tf-redshift-logging-test-bucket/*"
                },
                {
                    "Sid": "Get bucket policy needed for audit logging ",
                    "Effect": "Allow",
                    "Principal": {
                        "AWS": "${data.aws_redshift_service_account.main.arn}"
                    },
                    "Action": "s3:GetBucketAcl",
                    "Resource": "arn:aws:s3:::tf-redshift-logging-test-bucket"
                }
        ]
    }
    EOF
}
```

When dealing with so many different types, clear boundaries need to be established to ensure that unnecessary duplication doesn't happen. The only real exception to data duplication is caching.

With caching, you need to make sure that the data that you require is easily and quickly accessible, which will mean duplication, not necessarily of the raw data, but some of the most frequently accessed data.

Data transforms and caching layers can be used to provide necessary abstractions that support refactoring and cutover as necessary.

Logging

Don't use binary logs, stick with text, and try to adhere to standard formats if possible—it'll pay dividends in clarity. Don't log everything by default; you'll create a data lake that you won't know what to do with. Having too much data is as much of a problem as not having enough. Too much data can mask issues and reduces the amount of resolution—it's difficult to find the wood for the trees, so to speak.

Only increase log levels as needed and stdout and stderr channels where possible. These standard channels are available across the board and most, if not all, infrastructure engineers know what these are.

By using a consistent method to output your data, you cut down on possible issues with logging. Logs and errors should use consistent operating system mechanisms for local persistence—in the main these should be standard log files that can be aggregated by one of a number of services available.

Particularly useful is the CloudWatch for logging, but setting it up can be quite fiddly.

Firstly, you'll need to set up a log group as follows:

```
resource "aws_cloudwatch_log_group" "my-log-group" {
  name = "my-log-group"
  retention_in_days = "1"

  tags = {
    Environment = "production"
    Application = "serviceA"
  }
}
```

This just gives the log group a name and optionally how long to keep the log data, and allows you to add tags to assign various resources.

You'll then need to create some policies (IAM and resource) as follows:

```
data "aws_iam_policy_document" "my-logging-policy" {
  statement {
    actions = [
      "logs:*"
    ]

    resources = [
      "${aws_cloudwatch_log_group.my-log-group.arn}",
    ]
```

```
    principals {
      identifiers = ["my-domain.com"]
      type = "Service"
    }
  }
}

resource "aws_cloudwatch_log_resource_policy" "my-log-resource" {
  policy_document = "${data.aws_iam_policy_document.my-logging-
policy.json}"
  policy_name = "my-log-resource"
}
```

With these in place, you can now add log publishing options to your resources. An example of usage for Elasticsearch resources is as follows (different resources will set this up differently—please check on `https://www.terraform.io/docs/providers/aws/index.html` for specifics):

```
log_publishing_options {
  log_type = "INDEX_SLOW_LOGS"                    // Other log types
are available
  cloudwatch_log_group_arn = "${aws_cloudwatch_log_group.my-log-
resource.arn}"
  enabled = true
}
```

Once you have data flowing into your CloudWatch, you can set up metrics, events, alarms, and dashboards. These are too long to go into here, so I'll direct you to the following documentation:

- **Metrics**: `https://www.terraform.io/docs/providers/aws/r/cloudwatch_log_metric_filter.html`
- **Events**: `https://www.terraform.io/docs/providers/aws/r/cloudwatch_event_rule.html`
- **Alarms**: `https://www.terraform.io/docs/providers/aws/r/cloudwatch_metric_alarm.html`
- **Dashboard**: `https://www.terraform.io/docs/providers/aws/r/cloudwatch_dashboard.html`

Remote mechanisms for the long-term storage of logs need to have the same levels of availability and reliability as your customer-facing applications. Lost data, such as error traces, can increase your time to recovery. Incomplete or corrupt backups will jeopardize your recovery time objectives.

Summarized metrics

Do not perform your transforms before you persist your data—again using the *keep everything* mantra. Amazon provides very low-cost storage solutions and the trends are toward even lower prices in the future.

Throwing away your detailed data prevents you from answering questions you have yet to think of; it also prevents regenerating that same detailed data in case of catastrophic failure. We are not advocating duplication of unnecessary data points; capture deltas if you have limited bandwidth for transmission.

However, the cost saving of storing an averaged dataset (or a dataset using an equivocal mathematical method) in these situations where your systems can take advantage of AWS's low-cost networking, is probably less than the cost to your business of losing the data in case of failure. It also makes anomaly detection much more difficult in complex distributed systems. Furthermore, the greater your sample size, the more data you will have to feed data analysis, machine learning, or AI models.

Summary

AWS provides a huge number of alternatives for your data storage and processing needs.

Oftentimes, it is difficult to choose the right mix of services. Other times, the bright and shiny new toys distract from your product mission. Consider simple solutions in order to avoid getting stuck at a dead end. Use established patterns when possible and isolate your tests to minimize availability. Short iterative cycles in your data development process will allow you to avoid costly product mistakes in the same manner as Amazon.

Further reading

Check out this book for application and data related anti-patterns: https://www.amazon.com/SQL-Antipatterns-Programming-Pragmatic-Programmers/dp/1934356557

Other Books You May Enjoy

If you enjoyed this book, you may be interested in these other books by Packt:

Designing AWS Environments
Mitesh Soni, Wayde Gilchrist

ISBN: 978-1-78953-554-9

- Establish how to launch EC2 instances and log in
- Work with Linux and Windows instances
- Understand Amazon VPC networking creation with and without a wizard
- Design, create, and secure a Virtual Private Cloud
- Autoscale instances based on the increase and decrease in traffic
- Deploy applications in a highly available and fault-tolerant manner
- Load balance the requests with Elastic Load Balancing
- Make your applications highly available through load balancing, multi-AZ deployments, and auto scaling

Expert AWS Development
Atul V. Mistry

ISBN: 978-1-78847-758-1

- Learn how to get up and running with AWS Developer Tools.
- Integrate the four major phases in the Release Processes. Source, Build, Test and Production.
- Learn how to integrate Continuous Integration, Continuous Delivery, and Continuous Deployment in AWS.
- Make secure, scalable and fault tolerant applications.
- Understand different architectures and deploy complex architectures within minutes

Leave a review - let other readers know what you think

Please share your thoughts on this book with others by leaving a review on the site that you bought it from. If you purchased the book from Amazon, please leave us an honest review on this book's Amazon page. This is vital so that other potential readers can see and use your unbiased opinion to make purchasing decisions, we can understand what our customers think about our products, and our authors can see your feedback on the title that they have worked with Packt to create. It will only take a few minutes of your time, but is valuable to other potential customers, our authors, and Packt. Thank you!

Index

A

Access Control Lists (ACLs) 67, 135
access frequency 166
ACID 169
Advanced Persistent Threat (APT) 83
alarms
  about 223
  state, evaluating 225
  states 224
Amazon Certificate (ACM) 70
Amazon Comprehend
  AI 202
  anomaly detection 203
  forecasting 203
  prediction 203
Amazon Machine Images (AMI) 41
Amazon SageMaker 199
Amazon Web Services (AWS)
  about 10
  catalog 18
  cloud continuum 14
  code 12
  data 11
  Elastic Cloud Compute (EC2) 15
  free trials 17
  free trials, reference 16
  future 11
  history 10
  Infrastructure as a Service (IaaS) 13
  microservices 15
  Platform as a Service (PaaS) 13
  product 11
  reference 10
  Software as a Service (SaaS) 14
  utility computing 12
anti-patterns
  about 153
  monoliths 153
  networking 154
  scaling 154
  single points of failure 154
Anything as a Service (XaaS) 12
Application Load Balancer (ALB) 38
Application Programming Interfaces (APIs) 13
auto scaling
  about 57
  placement groups 58
automated canary analysis (ACA) pattern 113
Availability Zone (AZ)
  reference 54
AWS catalog
  about 18
  benefits 19
  cloud migration, benefits 19
AWS dashboards
  about 218
  alarm, adding 222
  alarm, removing 222
  creating 219
  dashboard, adding to favorites list 222
  graph, adding 220
  graph, editing 220
  graph, moving 220
  graph, removing 220
  graph, resizing 220
  graphs, linking 222
  graphs, unlinking 222
  metrics graphing, manually on CloudWatch
    dashboard 221
  resources, monitoring in multiple regions 222
  text widget, adding 221
  time range, changing 222
  time zone format, changing 222

AWS Terraform
  reference 30

B
batching 187, 190
best practices
  about 235
  lock-in 236
  tight coupling 235
Boto
  reference 12
business continuity
  about 128
  disaster recovery 131
  postmortems 132
  restore 130
  snapshots 128, 129, 130

C
caching
  about 191
  ElastiCache 191
CAP theorem
  Aurora and MySQL, setting up 170
  DynamoDB 172
  high availability 170
  high consistency 170
  partition tolerance 170
  unstructured data 172
capacity
  managing 218
change control board (CCB) 150
classification 205
Cloud Foundry 57
cloud migration, benefits
  for operations engineer 20
  for product owner 20
  for software engineer 19
cloud specific, responsibilities
  about 64
  compliance 65
  governance 64
  risk 65
  Virtual Private Cloud (VPC) 67
Cloud9 24, 27, 29

CloudFront 40
CloudHSM 75
CloudTrail 80, 176
CloudWatch
  about 211
  available metrics, searching for 213
  available metrics, viewing 212
  custom metrics, publishing 216
  events 81
  metric alarms, creating 212
  metric math, using 217
  metric statistics, getting 213, 215
  metrics, graphing 215
clustering 204
code
  about 24
  testing 105, 106, 109
CodeBuild
  about 90, 96
  build servers 105
  event-driven architecture 100, 104
  projects 96, 100
CodeCommit 31, 32
Cognito
  about 79
  identity pools 79
  user pools 79
compute models
  about 32
  instances 33
  raw 35
considerations 160
containers
  about 136
  elastic container service 138
  Kubernetes service, managed 139
  registry services 138
content delivery network (CDN) 40
cost
  managing 118
counterproductive processes
  control boards, changing 150
  exploring 149
  firefighting 151
  lift and shift 150

non-reproducibility 150
system uptime 151
credentials
  about 73
  certificates 74
  keys 74, 75

D

data
  changing 168
defense in depth
  in transit 66
  least privilege 66
  users 66
deployment strategies, exploring 112, 113
desilofication
  about 124
  balanced team 124
  product mindset 124
  self-service 125
  user-centered design 125
developer productivity 111, 112
dimensionality reduction 204
dimensions 163
Distributed Denial of Service (DDoS) 70
Domain Name Service (DNS) 36
Domain-Driven Design 153
durability 163
Dynamic Host Configuration Protocol (DHCP) 37
DynamoDB 172

E

Elastic Cloud Compute (EC2) 32
Elastic Container Registry (ECR) 138
Elastic Container Service (ECS) 32, 138
Elastic File System (EFS) 41
Elastic IP (EIP) 36
Elastic Kubernetes Service (EKS) 32
Elastic Load Balancing (ELB) 38, 51
ElasticSearch 175
Elemental MediaStore 178
EMR 179
environment
  testing 115, 116, 118
ETL 193

event stream processing
  about 192
  Athena (querying S3) 193
events 226

F

fault injection
  about 127
  embrace risk 128
  reliability testing 127
fault tolerance 57

G

gateways
  internet gateway 38
  NAT gateway 38
  VPN gateway (VGN) 38
General Data Protection Regulation (GDPR) 65
Git
  reference 24
Global Traffic Manager (GTM) 51, 53
graph databases
  about 181
  Neptune 181
  time series 183

H

hierarchical storage management 59, 60
high availability
  about 46
  regions 50
  top-level domain 46, 48
Hypertext Transport Protocol (HTTP) 38
Hystrix
  URL 155

I

IAM
  about 41, 76, 77
  instance profiles 78
  Security Token Service (STS) 41
  users 77
image recognition 206
Infrastructure as Code (IaC) 65

inheritance 65
instances, compute models
  about 33
  types 33
  usage 34
Integrated Development Environment (IDE) 12, 24
Internet of Things (IoT) 15
Internet Protocol (IP)
  about 36
  elastic IP 36
  IPv6 36
interpolate missing data (sparsity) 205
intrusion detection and prevention services
  shield 39
  Web Application Firewall (WAF) 39

K

Kinesis 196

L

L1 Norm Regularization 205
latency 165
Load Balancer (LB)
  about 38
  Application Load Balancer (ALB) 38
  Elastic Load Balancing (ELB) 38
  local traffic manager 39
load balancing
  about 51
  Availability Zone (AZ) 54
  Global Traffic Manager (GTM) 51, 53
  health checks 56
  Local Traffic Management (LTM) 55, 56
Local Traffic Management (LTM) 54, 55
lock in 152
logging
  about 80
  flow logs 81
  GuardDuty 83

M

machine learning
  about 199
  Amazon Comprehend - NLP 201
  Amazon SageMaker 199

clustering 204
Jupyter Notebook 201
Managed Streaming for Kafka (MSK) 186
measurement
  about 125
  agreements 127
  indicators 126
  objectives 126
Minimum Viable Products (MVP)
  reference 11
monoliths 153, 161
multiple environments
  using 115

N

Network Address Translation (NAT) 69
network interface controllers (NIC) 135
networking options
  about 35
  gateways 38
  Internet Protocol (IP) 36
  intrusion detection and prevention services 39
  Load Balancer (LB) 38
  Route 53 36
  Virtual Private Cloud 37

O

Open Container Initiative (OCI) 137

P

pattern recognition 206
patterns
  about 237
  logging 243
  polyglot persistence 238
  summarized metrics 245
performance
  optimizing 218
polyglot persistence
  about 174, 238
  Amazon Simple Queue Service (SQS) 239
  Athena 238
  DocumentDB 239
  DynamoDB 240
  ElastiCache 240

Redshift 241
  text 174
processes
  analysis paralysis 233
  building 232
  trash 233
Product Manager (PM) 124
products, analyzing
  about 210
  logging 210
  metrics 211

Q

queuing
  about 185
  MSK 186

R

raw, compute models
  about 35
  containers 35
  functions 35
read
  versus write 164
Recover TIme Objective (RTO) 130
Recovery Point Objective (RPO) 130
reduction
  about 132
  local development 132
Relational Data Services (RDS)
  about 163, 168
  CAP theorem 169
  transactional data 169
reliability 164
role-based access control (RBAC)
  about 76
  directory service 76
Route 53
  about 36
  DNS 36
  global traffic manager 36
  reference 46
rules 227

S

scaling, anti-patterns
  resilience 155
Security Token Service (STS) 41
self-service, facilitating
  about 113
  templates 114
serverless 139, 141, 142, 144
service discovery 147, 148
shared responsibilities
  about 64
  cloud specific 64
  defense 66
  inheritance 65
Silos 152
Simple Notification Service (SOA) 224
Simple Storage Service (S3) 179
Software Development Life Cycle (SDLC) 66
Software-Defined Networking (SDN) 135
source control 90
sparse data 168
SQL database 237
start of authority (SOA) 223
state
  versus dynamic 166
storage
  about 39
  Amazon Machine Images (AMI) 41
  CloudFront 40
  Elastic Block Storage 40
  Elastic File System (EFS) 41
  Ephemeral 40
  Simple Storage Solution (S3) 40
  sizing 167
streamed 167

T

targets 226
Terraform
  reference 24
Timestream 183
tracing 223
transforms
  about 193

Audio/video (mp4 to mp3) 194
CloudTrail 198
elastic transcoder 194, 196
Kinesis 196
Transport Layer Security (TLS) 64
trees 205

U

Uniform Resource Indicator (URI) 46
usage instances, compute models
   about 34
   dedicated 34
   shared 34
   spot or ephemeral 34

V

version control 152
vertical scaling
   versus horizontal scaling 161
Virtual Private Cloud (VPC)
   about 67
   application 70

network ACLs 68
obscurity 69
peering 37
routing 37
security groups 67
subnets 37
vulnerability scanning
   about 83
   buckets 84
   cloud environment 85
   code and functions 84
   containers 84
   instance-level scanning 83
   network 84

W

Web Application Firewall (WAF) 39
work flow
   considerations 160

X

X-Ray 223

Printed in Great Britain
by Amazon